Contents

The Use of Assessment Techniques by Applied Psychologists

P A U L A   S A C H S   W I S E

Western Illinois University

Wadsworth Publishing Company
Belmont, California
A Division of Wadsworth, Inc.

Psychology Editor: Kenneth King
Editorial Assistant: Cheri Peterson
Production Editor: Sandra Craig
Designer: MaryEllen Podgorski
Print Buyer: Karen Hunt
Copy Editor: Stephen Forsling
Compositor: Graphic Typesetting Service

Printed in the United States of America 49

1 2 3 4 5 6 7 8 9 10—93 92 91 90 89

Library of Congress Cataloging-in-Publication Data
Wise, Paula Sachs.
   The use of assessment techniques by applied psychologists.
   Bibliography: p.
   Includes index.
   1. Psychological tests.   2. Psychology, Applied.
I. Title.
BF176.W57 1989   153.9'3   88-17409
ISBN 0-534-09750-2

Preface

The major purpose of this book is to provide readers with insights into the ways in which professional psychologists conduct psychological assessments in a variety of applied settings. To me these are the most interesting, the most gratifying, and the most challenging aspects of psychological assessment. Unfortunately, psychological tests and measurement courses never mention many of these applications. Students may leave these classes with the mistaken impression that the study of psychological testing is boring, requiring the rote memorization of information about reliability, validity, and item analysis. Such information is important, but there is a lot more to testing.

Psychological assessment techniques can be both interesting and useful in providing psychologists with insights into the behaviors and experiences of their clients. I have used two approaches to convey as realistic and dynamic a view of psychological assessment as possible. First, I have described the processes that applied psychologists employ with assessment techniques. How do clinical, counseling, industrial/organizational, and school psychologists use tests and other assessment procedures in their work to help them learn about their clients? Where do such procedures fit into the professional roles and functions of these psychologists? Following these descriptions, I have provided examples and case studies illustrating the specific assessment-related procedures and techniques that a psychologist might employ on the job.

This book originates from feelings of frustration I have had as a student, as a professor, and as a coordinator of a graduate program. As an undergraduate, I sat through many classes without the slightest inkling of what I actually wanted to do when I graduated. I knew I enjoyed working with people, particularly young people, and I enjoyed the university environment sufficiently to want to continue my studies in a graduate program, but I had no knowledge about what options were available to me. Quite by chance I stumbled on the field of school psychology. The notion that I could combine my fascination with psychology with my desire to work with children and that I could obtain gainful employment with a master's degree seemed almost too good to be true.

As a faculty member, I have taught many sections of psychological tests and measurements. In my discussions with students, I have been occasionally appalled at the lack of information they display about careers in their major field. Whenever possible, I try to use questions to encourage students to think about certain issues. For example: If you were developing a new psychological test, how could you guard against its being administered and interpreted by an unqualified person? What major decisions have you made on the basis of psychological tests? Often discussions based on such questions evolve into discussions of the practice of psychology. Students will ask, How does a person get to be a psychologist in private practice? How long do you have to go to school to administer psychological tests? What kind of psychologist would administer an MMPI and what would you know from the results? Who are the people who present data about psychological tests in courtrooms? In my classes I am more than willing to spend time discussing these questions. But I find it surprising that juniors and seniors majoring in psychology know so little about the actual practice of psychology.

Finally, as the coordinator of a master's-level graduate program, I have been increasingly discouraged by the number of senior majors who have never heard of any field of psychology except clinical psychology. Clinical psychology is a fine area, but it can only absorb so many students, and admission into doctoral-level training programs in clinical psychology is fiercely competitive. In addition, the roles and functions of clinical psychologists are not for everyone.

I hope that after reading this book, readers will be aware of several fields of psychology. My goals for this book are as follows:
1. To begin to fill the gap between the theoretical information offered by traditional tests and measurement textbooks and the practical information that is often neglected.
2. To provide readers with a view of psychological assessment techniques in applied settings, where they are most often used.
3. To provide readers with some insights into psychological assessment, an important function of many careers in psychology.

If you are a junior or senior psychology student, you have probably begun to think about careers. Perhaps you hope that learning about psychological testing will provide you with employable skills. If that is so, you may be feeling rather disappointed and frustrated. You still have no marketable skills, and you are not even certain what you will need to obtain a job as a psychologist.

This book will not provide you with marketable skills. If you read it carefully, however, you should have a better idea of the kinds of skills (at least the assessment-related kinds) applied psychologists need to work in four areas of specialization.

Faculty members may have some questions about where to include the book in an already full undergraduate curriculum. I see at least three appropriate places. My original idea was to use the book as a supplement in introductory courses in psychological tests and measurement. It is sufficiently brief that psychology majors in these courses might be willing to read it for little, if any, extra credit. Many of the topics presented here lend themselves to class discussions and student presentations. Discussing the book in the last weeks of class could pull together much of the traditional material already covered. If you perceive psychological tests and measurements as too overwhelming a subject for one course, offering a follow-up course for students considering graduate work in an applied area of psychology might be a realistic way to discuss additional topics included in this book.

Teachers might also recommend the book to their psychology club or Psi Chi chapter as part of a lecture or discussion series. Guest speakers in each of the four applied areas could present supplementary information.

If your department offers a seminar on training and employment strategies for psychology majors, this book could supplement its reading list. Much of the information here describing the actual functioning of applied psychologists is difficult to find in other sources. If your department does not offer such a course, counselors who advise students about career opportunities might familiarize themselves with the contents of this book and recommend it to students who are headed for graduate school.

Acknowledgments

Many people have contributed to this book. Several of my colleagues in the psychology department at Western Illinois University have reviewed chapters or have helped me to clarify issues, including Scott Huebner, Al Richert, Alan Witt, Frank Fulkerson, and Charlie Potkay. I also wish to acknowledge the various individuals and committees on campus that granted me one of the university's much sought-after sabbatical leaves to work on this project.

In addition, I would like to thank Ken King, the editor at Wadsworth, who has encouraged me in my writing and coordinated the review process. The reviewers are worthy of thanks for their kind words and constructive criticisms: Gwyneth M. Boodoo, Texas A & M University; William J. Gnagey, Illinois State University; Barry Mallinger, Radford University; and Gil Sax, University of Washington.

Ms. Donna Leach must be mentioned for using her meticulous word-processing skills on countless drafts of each chapter of the manuscript. She never became impatient when I asked her for "just one more change."

My husband, Dan, and my son, Ben, have put up with me throughout the entire process. Along with my parents they have encouraged me and offered love, moral support, and unconditional positive regard in all of my professional accomplishments. Thank you all!

Paula Sachs Wise

Introduction to Applied Psychological Assessment

Psychological tests can be defined as instruments that attempt to measure a variety of human characteristics and behaviors. Such tests are merely tools that are neither helpful nor harmful in and of themselves. The controversies over psychological tests are based on their applications. For example, how will the test results be used? Are the decisions based on test results appropriate in light of the test content, the validity and reliability data, and the standardization sample?

The purpose of this book is to provide insights into the ways in which assessments are conducted in real settings by professional psychologists. Most readers of this book probably either are enrolled in undergraduate classes in psychological tests and measurements or have taken such a course. In the typical course, students read about and attend lectures on norms, reliability, validity, item analysis, individually administered tests of intelligence, group tests, tests for special populations, achievement tests, personality tests, interest inventories, vocational aptitude tests, and so forth. Professors in such courses usually address the ethical aspects of testing, the history of testing, and the future of testing. Familiarity with such information will enable readers to derive maximum benefit from this book.

On the other hand, many introductory courses in psychological tests and measurements devote little if any time to discussing the applications of test data to the practice of psychology. These applications are undoubtedly the most intriguing and potentially the most gratifying but are also the most frustrating aspects of psychological assessment. The applications of assessment data have tremendous impact on all of our lives and have sparked controversy and even legal battles. The applications of assessment data to the practice of psychology form the basis of this book.

How Do Psychological Tests Affect Our Lives?

From the time children enter school—and sometimes even before that—they take tests. Some of these tests are written, administered, and scored by individual teachers. Such "teacher-made tests" are used to evaluate each student's progress, to determine if a particular student is ready to move on to other materials, to assign grades, and to measure the class's progress as a whole to provide feedback to the teacher. No doubt everyone reading this book can recall instances when teacher-made tests seemed fair and times when they seemed unfair. From a student's perspective, fair tests meet the criteria for validity. That is, they measure what they are supposed to measure at an appropriate level of difficulty. Unfair tests in students' words, are "ambiguous" or "picky," "didn't ask what I expected," or are "too long," "too specific," or "too difficult."

Moving from teacher-made tests to psychological tests, we shift from measures of course-specific content to more general measures of behavior and experience developed with extreme sensitivity to psychometric properties. Elementary school students take group tests of ability; junior high school students take a variety of aptitude and achievement tests; high school students take vocational aptitude tests and precollege aptitude tests. Somewhere along the line students may be given an individually administered psychological test for a variety of reasons. In the schools, individual and group psychological tests may help to determine everything from entrance into special classes for the handicapped to admission into programs for gifted and talented youngsters. In other words, many potentially life-shaping decisions are made about children and adolescents based on the application of the results of psychological tests.

Young people are not the only ones evaluated through the use of psychological tests. Individuals accused of committing crimes are evaluated to determine if they are "not guilty by reason of insanity" or competent to stand trial. Businesses and industries assess prospective employees to determine if they have the appropriate skills, aptitudes, and occasionally even personality characteristics for a specific job. People with a variety of personal difficulties may be tested as one portion of the psychological services they receive.

Because so many important decisions are based on results of psychological tests, the designers of these tests must be extremely careful to develop instruments that are psychometrically sound. However, responsibility does not stop with the test designer. Anyone who uses such a test must be ethical as well as knowledgeable in test selection, administration, and interpretation practices. The actual administration of a test may in fact be the easiest part of the whole process.

Anyone with a reasonable amount of intelligence, good reading and writing skills, and the ability to follow directions can be trained in a relatively brief time to perform these tasks properly. Building rapport with the person taking the test is not necessarily restricted to those with advanced degrees. (Some people might even argue that an advanced degree hinders the establishment of a relationship.) Some psychological tests designed for computerized administration and scoring remove the psychologist from these functions altogether.

Why then is the use of psychological assessment limited to those with graduate degrees in psychology? The reasons reflect the very nature of the difference between testing and assessment. The term **testing** refers to the mechanical acts of administering and scoring a psychological test; these are merely two aspects of the total assessment process. **Assessment**, on the other hand, is viewed more broadly as a process that enables the psychologist to identify, diagnose, and remedy an individual's difficulties. Nearly anyone can be taught to administer and score a test in a relatively short time, but assessment involves higher-level skills—the so-called "clinical skills" that can only be acquired through extensive training and experience.

An individual turns to a psychologist for assistance in solving a problem of some sort. The problem can involve the referring agent or a business associate, a child in a classroom, a roommate, or a family member. The psychologist must identify the problem, find out what factors are contributing to the problem, and suggest strategies for coping with or eliminating the problem. Assessment is part of each of these functions, testing may or may not be involved.

The Process of Assessment

The process of assessment has always seemed to me to be a specialized application of the scientific method. The creative parts of the scientific method involve formulating the question, designing the means of addressing the question, and interpreting the results with all available information taken into consideration. Running the actual experiment is a small though admittedly critical step in this process. So it is with assessment and testing. From a general standpoint, assessment involves four steps:

1. Formulating the question: Why is this woman unable to hold a job? Why is this child having difficulty paying attention? Why did this teenager attempt to commit suicide?

2. Addressing the question: Gathering background information and assessing the level of present functioning.

3. Interpreting the results: What is causing the individual to behave this way?

4. Making recommendations: What can be done to bring about change?

A logical question at this point in the discussion might be: What sources of information and procedures, in addition to actual test data, does the psychologist use in addressing the client's difficulties? A list of such items would include, but not be limited to, the following: referral information, interview data, previous records and reports, observational data, testing, reporting assessment results, and follow-up.

Referral Information

Most schools, clinics, hospitals, and other agencies have some kind of standardized referral or intake form that must be completed before any other procedures are begun. The information on such forms varies, depending on the agency. Nearly all forms ask the client's name, address, phone number, date of birth, and gender, as well as the name of the person making the referral (if other than the client) and the relationship of the person making the referral (parent, teacher, neighbor, social worker, and so on). A brief description of the presenting problem would also be a standard question. Often the intake forms will contain a checklist of some common types of problems (for instance, depression, anxiety, interpersonal relationships, and substance abuse), along with a space for the person who completes the intake form to elaborate on the nature of the difficulty.

The information provided on the referral form should, either explicitly or implicitly, contain a **referral question**. In other words, after reading the referral form, the psychologist should have some notion about why the referral was initiated and what questions are to be answered. The referral question may be formulated by the referring agent or the psychologist or both. At this point the psychologist begins to formulate some tentative hypotheses regarding the nature and extent of the problem. Subsequent steps in the assessment process enable the psychologist to reject, accept, or refine these initial hypotheses.

● ● ● ● ● ●

EXAMPLE 1.1 A

A counseling psychologist employed by a large corporation receives a referral form regarding a new employee. The form has been completed by the employee's immediate supervisor, who is frustrated by the employee's "frequent tardiness, absenteeism, and illnesses. When he is here and healthy he does good work, but his frequent lateness and absences make it hard to count on him. I have to readjust the work schedule and give his work to the others. That makes the others angry at me."

What hypotheses can you come up with to explain the employee's behavior? (My first guess would probably be an alcohol abuse problem, with marital or family problems a close second.) What might you do next to test your hypotheses? ●

Interview Data

To acquire as much information as possible about the client, the psychologist may interview the client along with some significant individuals in the client's environment (for example, parents or other family members, friends, teachers, past or present employers, co-workers, and classmates). Each of these individuals may have a unique perspective as to the nature, the manifestations, and even the causes of the client's problems. For instance, a mother may feel that her teenage son, Don, has become sulky and withdrawn; a teacher may feel that Don is just going through a typical phase of adolescence; a classmate may suspect that Don is using drugs; whereas a close friend may know that Don is extremely worried about his chances of being accepted at a certain college and that he has begun drinking quite heavily.

Of course, before such interviews occur, the psychologist must obtain the client's permission in writing. In the case of children, parental permission must be obtained.

The psychologist may gather data through a structured format, in which a preselected set of questions is used, or through a less-structured, clinical format, in which the discussions are directed by the interviewee's responses. A structured format may include the following questions:

- Are you employed?

- If so, by whom?

- How long have you worked there?

- Tell me a little bit about your work.

- Do you like what you do?

- Are you married?

- Do you have any children?

- How old are they?

- What are their names?

- What do you like to do when you're not working?

- Do you have any health problems?

- How did you hear about this clinic?

- What brings you here at this time?

- Have you ever gone to a psychologist before?

- What kinds of questions do you have for me?

Even the most structured interview format must be flexible enough to allow for differences in clients. A sixteen-year-old having difficulty in school would probably be asked about school rather than work and would probably not be asked "Are you married?" Still, a structured interview technique allows the psychologist to obtain vital information through client observation in a relatively standardized setting.

A less-structured, clinical format may begin with a statement such as, "Tell me about yourself and what brings you here today." As the client talks, the psychologist nods or comments to indicate interest, to demonstrate acceptance of the client, and to provide the client with reinforcement. Also, the psychologist periodically asks for additional information to clarify a statement. The unstructured interview format enables the psychologist to observe the client's reactions to an intentionally ambiguous situation.

● ● ● ● ● ●

EXAMPLE 1.1 B

Following an unstructured interview with Jim (the employee), the psychologist has learned that Jim is very unhappy with his life. He believes that he is at "the end of the line"—that there is no chance for him to advance and that he will be performing this rather menial job "till the day I die." Jim is forty-five years old, is divorced, and has two children, a seventeen-year-old boy and a nineteen-year-old girl. His ex-wife and children live in another state, and he rarely sees or hears from them. When they are together, "we have nothing much to say to each other."

Jim admitted that he does "drink a lot of beer, but I'm not an alcoholic. I don't really need to drink, I just like beer." When asked how much he drinks, Jim said, "About a six-pack a day, not much more usually."

My initial hypotheses of an alcohol or family problem or both seem to be at least somewhat substantiated by the interview data. What might you do to clarify the problem further? Many psychologists seek out other sources of information to aid in their understanding of the client's difficulties. Some of these sources are discussed in the following sections. ●

Previous Records and Reports

Often a great deal can be learned from collecting and reviewing existing information. The psychologist who receives copies of four previous psychological reports and five group-administered tests of ability all stating that "Richard's IQ is well within the normal range" probably does not need to spend a couple of hours administering yet another IQ test unless there is reason to suspect a change. Similarly, reviewing an ophthalmologist's report that "Rhoda should wear her glasses at all times" combined with the teacher's report that "Rhoda does not wear glasses" may explain why Rhoda is having trouble completing her work in school. As with all of the other sources of information, the psychologist needs written permission from the client (or client's parent or guardian) to see most of these previous records and reports.

Some psychologists hesitate to read previous reports prior to meeting a client. They believe that the so-called expectancy effect will have a strong influence on their initial perceptions of the individual and prefer instead to form their own impressions, then read what others have written. Other psychologists avidly read all available information about a client in advance, believing that the more historical data they have, the better use they can make of their time with the client. Both methods have merit, but neither is best under all circumstances. At the very least, an awareness of the influence of "expectancy effects" is mandatory for those choosing to read reports before meeting a client.

● ● ● ● ● ●

EXAMPLE 1.1 C

Reviewing Jim's records provided the psychologist with some useful information. Jim's previous employer's letter of recommendation contained the following paragraph: "Jim is a bright, hardworking individual. He takes instruction well, keeps pretty much to himself, and does not cause any trouble. The only problem I have had with him is his frequent absences. It's hard to plan anything not knowing if he'll be here. When he's here, he's a model employee."

In the past five years, Jim has held six different jobs. All of the previous employers cited "job absence" as their only complaint about Jim's performance. He was hired in his present position because he was the only qualified applicant. At the time of Jim's hiring, the personnel director spoke to Jim about his absences. Jim responded "I've had some personal problems, but I think they're behind me now. I'm ready to settle down and work."

What would you have done if you were the personnel director? As the psychologist in this case, what would you do next? ●

Observational Data

If a teacher told you, "One of my students is a real behavior problem," could you tell which student it is merely by observing in the classroom for an hour? How about by observing on the playground? Can you learn anything about a man by observing him at home with his family? What can you learn about a woman by watching her at work?

Most psychological evaluations are conducted under nearly ideal conditions—few distractions and a one-examiner-to-one-client ratio. Such evaluations provide psychologists with the opportunity to observe the client's optimal performance. It is important to note that the problem behavior rarely occurs under such ideal conditions.

Teachers and other consumers of psychological services can become extremely annoyed when a psychologist tells them, "I don't see any evidence of hyperactivity. Joe responded to all of my questions and only needed an occasional reminder to remain seated." Put Joe in a classroom with twenty-seven other children and one teacher, however, and Joe is "climbing the walls." At home, Joe has never finished anything he has started, nor has he ever followed a direction without reminders or threats.

Most people react in different ways to different situations. A child who has table manners described as "gross" by his mother may be described as "a polite and neat youngster" by his friend's mother. Part of the discrepancy can be accounted for by differences in the person's behavior based on the setting. Another factor to take into consideration is "observer-bias" or "observer-interpretation." A careful and conscientious employee to one employer may be a slow and labored worker to a second employer.

It is important to gather as much observational data as possible whenever appropriate to gain a more thorough understanding of every client. Observing under a variety of circumstances (at work, at home, at lunch, and at school) is extremely interesting but often neither practical nor necessary.

● ● ● ● ● ●

EXAMPLE 1.1 D

In Jim's case, the psychologist chose not to observe directly. Instead, the psychologist asked Josie, Jim's supervisor, to keep an accurate chart of Jim's work record during the next two weeks. Josie was to mark Jim's presence or absence, time of arrival, physical complaints, and excuses on the chart.

Week One

Monday —	absent from work (had the flu)
Tuesday —	forty-five minutes late (alarm didn't go off)
—	complained of headache
Wednesday —	ten minutes late (bus was late)
—	complained of tiredness
Thursday —	ten minutes late (bus was late)
Friday —	two minutes late (no excuses)
—	complained of headache and backache

Week Two

Monday —	two hours late (didn't feel well)
—	complained of headache and dizziness
Tuesday —	absent from work (too tired)

Wednesday — ten minutes late (bus)
— complained of tiredness
Thursday — ten minutes late (bus was late)
Friday — two minutes late (no excuses)

Josie said that this two-week pattern was "pretty typical" of Jim's behavior since he had been hired.

What have we accomplished by gathering these data? Why did it seem more appropriate for someone on-the-job, rather than the psychologist, to gather the information? What should be done next? •

Testing

After gathering some or all of the information just described, testing may or may not be an appropriate next step. Testing allows the psychologist to observe a client's work style in a relatively standardized setting. It also provides the psychologist with quantifiable data about the client's abilities and achievement. Testing can be thought of as a shortcut—a quick and orderly way of gathering information about a client. But testing is not a panacea, and it is doubtful that simply taking a psychological test has ever "cured" anyone of anything.

Testing can also be a rapport-builder for clients who may be uncomfortable or apprehensive about spending time with a psychologist. The structured nature of testing is often a much better ice-breaker than an open-ended question such as, "Tell me about yourself, and what brings you here today?" In addition, we may lose sight of the fact that clients sometimes need time to observe the people who are observing them. Testing may provide the opportunity for this observation as well. Many people view psychology in general and psychologists in particular with great suspicion. We may be perceived as "mind-readers" or as possessors of mystical curative powers. Clients may need to see the psychologist as a person before they feel comfortable talking about their thoughts and feelings.

The testing process can be divided into three independent steps: selection, administration, and scoring. The first step—choosing one or more test instruments—may sound easier than it actually is. Hundreds of psychological tests are available, with multiple tests for any characteristic or ability imaginable. In selecting a test, the psychologist must keep in mind the following information:

- The psychometric characteristics of the test: Validity, reliability, norms, and so on.

- The age, race, ethnic background, and gender of the client: How similar is the client to the group on which the test was normed?

- The referral question: Will this test tell me what I need to know to answer the question(s)?

- The logistics: Do I have the time, the materials, and the proper environment for this test?

- The right "kind" of client: Is the client able to see, hear, read, write, and follow directions well enough to take this test?

- The right "kind" of examiner: Does the psychologist have the proper background and training to administer, score, and interpret this test?

After selecting one or more tests, the psychologist must administer the tests. Test administration necessitates that the examiner possesses the professional credentials specified in the test manual. The psychologist also has the ethical obligation to be thoroughly familiar with all testing procedures. Most psychological tests require skilled examiners who know when a response is right or wrong, when to question further, what to say to introduce a specific test, when to stop testing, how much time to allow per item, and so forth. For a test to yield meaningful results, these standardized procedures must be *strictly* followed. Test administrators usually find it helpful to practice giving a test (usually on a "somewhat" willing friend or relative) before using the test professionally. It should be noted that the test results gained from such practice sessions are usually not shared with the volunteer.

After the test instruments are administered, the examiner may devote a considerable amount of time to scoring and interpreting the results. Some tests can be scored rapidly either by hand or with the help of a computer. These easily scored tests usually have answers that are either "right" or "wrong," and the numbers of right and wrong answers are merely tallied.

Other tests take more time, but the experienced examiner may still score them fairly quickly. The best examples of such tests are the Wechsler Scales of Intelligence. Questions on the verbal section of the Wechsler Intelligence Scale for Children—Revised (WISC-R) or the Wechsler Adult Intelligence Scale—Revised (WAIS-R) require definitions of words and other frequently lengthy verbal responses that must be scored carefully. The tests provide "right " and "wrong" answer samples along with general guidelines for scoring. They also offer answers that are questionable, requiring elaboration from the person taking the test. Although an occasional response may stump even the most experienced test administrator, usually the examiner can make the distinction between right, questionable, or wrong responses fairly quickly and easily.

Imagine the amount of time involved in scoring tests such as the Rorschach or the Thematic Apperception Test (TAT). Such projective instruments are deliberately designed to be ambiguous, and the client's responses to the stimuli are often quite lengthy. In addition, multiple scoring systems are available to evaluate responses. The time spent in scoring such a test would be considerable even for the experienced examiner. Although projective instruments have many opponents, the advocates of such tests argue that the time spent in administering and scoring the tests helps in understanding the client.

• • • • • •

EXAMPLE 1.1E

The psychologist working with Jim decided not to administer any psychological tests at this time. In Jim's case, the psychologist decided that developing a behavioral contract with Jim might work to control Jim's absences and lateness. Because of his excessive absences, Jim's pay would be docked for every hour or fraction of an hour that he was not on-the-job. (The amount of money would be computed based on his salary.) If he missed more than 5 percent of his expected work time in the next month, Jim would be fired.

Other psychologists might have chosen to administer one or more tests to Jim to increase their understanding of his problem. Based on your knowledge of available psychological tests, what test(s) would you have administered to Jim? One test-related possibility to consider in Jim's case might be a referral for vocational testing to determine avenues Jim might wish to pursue instead of his current self-described "end-of-the-line" job. •

Reporting Assessment Results

There are two traditional methods for reporting the results of psychological assessments. The first method consists of writing a formal report; the second entails sharing the results in a conference or meeting with the appropriate individuals. Often, information is shared in both ways. Written reports vary so much from psychologist to psychologist that it is extremely difficult to make generalizations about them. S. Shellenberger (1982) summarized the professional literature to answer the question "What makes a psychological report effective?" Based on her research, she listed six characteristics of effective psychological reports (pp. 52–53). Such reports:

1. *"Answer the referral question"*: A report can be beautifully written with brilliant and insightful observations, but if it does not tell the reader "Why can't Johnny read?" or "What can we do about Melanie's low self-esteem?" little has been accomplished.

2. *"Describe behavior "*: The psychologist should not simply state that "Bobbie is a very angry young woman." The specific behaviors that led to such a conclusion should be described.

3. *"Are written in a clear, precise, straightforward manner"*: It is probably safe to say that no psychological report will ever earn a psychologist a Nobel Prize for Literature. Flowery prose is out! Technical terms are okay if the report is intended only for another psychologist. When the "consumer" of the report is a client, a parent, a teacher, or an employer, technical jargon is inappropriate. The purpose of a report is to explain the results of assessment to the reader. The purpose is *not* to confuse the reader thoroughly or to attempt to impress the reader with the size of the psychologist's vocabulary.

4. *"Synthesize and integrate information"*: Reports should go beyond merely listing any tests administered and the specific scores obtained. An effort should be made to tie the information together and, if necessary, to explain any inconsistencies. In addition, the psychologist should explain why a particular test was selected.

5. *"Provide recommendations that are explicit, specific, and implementable"*: Most psychological testing provides the psychologist with the opportunity to assess a client quickly. Often psychological assessments merely confirm what the client, parent, teacher, or employer already know. Usually the client is saying, "I know I have a problem. What should I do about it?" For this reason the recommendations section of a psychological report is the section that has the greatest likelihood of actually being read.

6. *"Are timely"*: The longer the interval between the assessment and the receipt of the report the less likely the report will ever be read.

Psychological reports are important for several reasons: They provide the writer and the reader with a written record of the assessment procedures, they afford psychologists the opportunity to organize their observations and perceptions, and they allow readers the chance to examine and reexamine the information provided at their own pace.

Psychological reports are usually *not* as important as face-to-face conferences in which the results of assessment are shared. Quite frankly, many psychological reports are filed away before anyone reads them. Often, the summary and the recommendations section may be the only sections that receive attention. In a conference, however, the psychologist has a far greater opportunity to present the results of assessment and to elicit participants' help in offering and implementing recommendations. Success in a conference depends to a large extent on the psychologist's interpersonal communication skills. Characteristics such as openness, intelligence, honesty, ability to accept the feelings of others, warmth, and respect are vital to its success. These characteristics are conveyed in many ways—what is said, the way in which it is said, facial expressions, body language, and even the arrangement of furniture in the conference room.

● ● ● ● ● ●

EXAMPLE 1.1 F

The psychologist met with Jim and with Josie, Jim's supervisor, to explain the intervention plan (Example 1.1 E, above) and discuss its implementation. The intervention plan was written up in the form of a contract and

Jim and Josie were asked to sign the contract. The tone of the meeting was positive and productive. The psychologist presented the plan as a "second chance" for Jim, and Jim seemed genuinely motivated to improve his performance. Josie complimented Jim on his work and told him she hoped he would succeed because she would hate to lose him. •

Follow-Up

Too often psychologists complete all of the steps listed and then move on to another "case" without so much as a backward glance to find out whether their recommendations were implemented and, if so, whether they were helpful. The follow-up phase of assessment is vital to the process for several reasons: It tells the clients that someone cares about them, it gives the psychologist and the client a chance to modify or change a recommended strategy, and it provides much-needed feedback to psychologists about the usefulness of their recommendations. Frequently, the only time a client contacts a psychologist is when the recommendations are *not* working. As long as things are satisfactory, the client will not make contact. Psychologists need positive reinforcement as much as anyone, and systematic follow-up procedures may help. Finally, systematic follow-up can lead to desperately needed information about the utility of intervention procedures. Presently very limited research is available about which interventions work with specific clients and circumstances.

• • • • • •

EXAMPLE 1.1 G

The psychologist checked with Jim and with Josie once a week during the month-long duration of the contract. Jim's performance improved gradually over the four-week period. Jim also began, on his own initiative, to see a counselor at the local community mental health center to come to terms with the "personal problems" that were troubling him. Although Jim is still not always on time for work, his absences are under control, and he has become a much more dependable employee. •

The seven procedures listed and described in this section—referral information, interview data, previous records and reports, observational data, testing, reporting assessment results, and follow-up—comprise the assessment process. Not all of these procedures are necessary or even appropriate in all situations for all types of applied psychologists. The applications and modifications of these steps will be presented in the chapters of this book devoted to the four applied areas of psychology (Chapters 3 through 6).

Organization of the Remainder of This Book

For clarity the various applications of psychology are divided into the four traditional "applied areas" of psychology. Chapter 2 offers brief descriptions of the four applied areas and provides background information for Chapters 3 through 6. Chapter 3 deals with the clinical psychologist's uses of psychological assessment data; Chapter 4 concerns counseling psychology; Chapter 5 is about industrial/organizational psychology, and Chapter 6 discusses school psychology.

Other authors of books related to applied psychology have chosen alternative organizational structures. For example, material may be organized by setting—e.g., private practice, university counseling centers, psychiatric hospitals, public schools, or businesses and industries. Population can be another organizing device, including psychologists who work with children, with adults, with people who have disabilities, with the elderly, and so forth.

If you look at the list of divisions within the American Psychological Association, you can see the dilemma (see Table 1.1). Recently I was asked on a survey to list the division with which I align myself most closely. I quickly marked Division 16, School Psychology, because that is my strongest professional allegiance. On the other hand, I am a dues-paying member of Division 2, Teaching of Psychology, because I am a professor interested in teaching-related issues; I am a member of Division 35, Psychology of Women, because I am a woman concerned with women's issues; and I am a member of Division 37, Child, Youth, and Family Services, because I am interested in these issues as well. In fact, it would probably be difficult to find a member of Division 16 who is not interested in child, youth, and family issues, but interest in such issues is by no means limited to school psychologists.

While writing the four chapters on the applied areas, I found some information that did not fit conveniently within any of the areas. Chapters 7 and 8 meet this need. Chapter 7 presents several of the most controversial issues concerning the uses and abuses of psychological assessment practices and procedures. Included in the chapter is a section about the increasing trend toward computerization in every portion of the assessment process. Chapter 8 is an attempt to tie together some loose ends, to draw some tentative conclusions from the previous seven chapters, and to address the future of psychological assessment based on past and present practices.

T A B L E 1.1 Divisions of the American Psychological Association

Number/Name	Total Membership
1. General Psychology	5,523
2. Teaching of Psychology	1,892
3. Experimental Psychology	1,490
5. Evaluation and Measurement	1,339
6. Physiological and Comparative	806
7. Developmental Psychology	1,307
8. Personality and Social	3,187
9. Society for the Psychological Study of Social Issues	2,811
10. Psychology and the Arts	449
12. Clinical Psychology	5,678
13. Consulting Psychology	933
14. Industrial and Organizational	2,502
15. Educational Psychology	2,049
16. School Psychology	2,264
17. Counseling Psychology	2,651
18. Psychologists in Public Service	965
19. Military Psychology	645
20. Adult Development and Aging	1,145
21. Applied Experimental and Engineering Psychologists	617
22. Rehabilitation Psychology	1,001
23. Consumer Psychology	419
24. Theoretical and Philosophical Psychology	585
25. Experimental Analysis of Behavior	1,274
26. History of Psychology	728
27. Community Psychology	1,596
28. Psychopharmacology	1,075
29. Psychotherapy	4,665
30. Psychological Hypnosis	1,429
31. State Psychological Association Affairs	533
32. Humanistic Psychology	791
33. Mental Retardation	834
34. Population and Environmental Psychology	467
35. Psychology of Women	2,229
36. Psychologists Interested in Religious Issues	1,287
37. Child, Youth, and Family Services	1,474
38. Health Psychology	2,704
39. Psychoanalysis	2,177
40. Clinical Neuropsychology	2,117
41. Psychology and Law Society	1,075
42. Psychologists in Independent Practice	5,090
43. Family Psychology	1,576
44. Society for the Psychological Study of Lesbian and Gay Issues	554

From the *1986 APA Membership Register* (1986). American Psychological Association, Washington, D.C.

IDEAS FOR FURTHER STUDY

1. Think about the psychological tests you have taken at various times in your life—achievement, aptitude, vocational, and so forth. Why did you take them? What results were shared with you or with your parents? How did taking the tests influence your life? How did you feel about taking the tests?

2. Go back to your high school and ask to see the results of any psychological tests you took as a student there.

3. What ethical questions are associated with each step of the assessment process?

4. In Table 1.1, APA Divisions 4 and 11 are not listed. Find out what they were and what happened to them.

5. When was each of the divisions founded? How does the development of the APA reflect the history of psychology or the history of social changes in America or both?

6. What are the various categories of membership status in the APA? How does a person qualify for each category?

CHAPTER 2

The Fields of Applied Psychology

Students majoring in psychology are frequently asked (especially by their parents), "What can you *do* with a degree in psychology?" This is not a simple question to address. Admittedly, psychology, as an undergraduate field of study, usually does not provide specific career preparation. Students majoring in an area such as education or accounting typically graduate and seek jobs in their chosen fields. Students majoring in psychology, on the other hand, graduate with a less-defined but perhaps broader set of skills. Recent surveys indicate that individuals with bachelor's degrees in psychology do find jobs (Wise, Smith, & Fulkerson, 1983; Ware & Meyer, 1981) and that many of the jobs appear to be at least indirectly related to training in psychology (for example, social services, education, and management).

Of course, mere possession of a bachelor's degree in psychology does not qualify someone to be a psychologist. That title is reserved for those with extensive advanced training and appropriate credentials. The nature of those credentials as well as the amount of training required have been hotly debated issues among practitioners.

Who Is a Psychologist?

A recent article (Stapp, Tucker, & VandenBos, 1985) in *American Psychologist*, a journal of the American Psychological Association (APA), used the term *psychological personnel* to include "all those who have a doctoral or master's degree in psychology or who are currently working in psychology" (p. 1319). This article, which reports the results of a census of psychological personnel, concludes that there were 102,101 people who fit the definition of psychological personnel in the United States as of mid-1983. Of the 80,000-plus people who returned census questionnaires, the largest group (38 percent) listed clinical psychology as their major field. School psychologists accounted for 13.1 percent of the total; counseling psychologists, for 11.7 percent; educational psychologists, for 6.3 percent; and industrial/organizational psychologists accounted for 4.7 percent of the total. Two thirds (66.7 percent) of survey respondents held doctorate degrees, while 28.2 percent held master's degrees. The remaining 5.1 percent either checked "other" or did not specify their highest degree.

Examining the percentages and the actual numbers of psychological personnel employed in the four areas traditionally considered to be the "applied" areas of psychology—clinical, counseling, industrial/organizational, and school—we find that 67.5 percent of the respondents (more than 54,000 people) considered one of these four areas as their major field.

The Entry-Level Degree Debate

Are all of these 54,000 people psychologists? This question reflects the long-running debate over the entry-level or minimum qualifications needed by individuals wishing to use the title "psychologist." In the study just reported, "psychological personnel" included all those with master's or doctoral degrees in psychology or those working in psychology. According to an American Psychological Association statement in 1977, however, the title "professional psychologist," along with its many variations (for instance, clinical, counseling, industrial/organizational and school psychologist), is "reserved for those who have completed a doctoral training program in psychology in a university, college, or professional school of psychology that is APA or regionally accredited. Only people who meet these qualifications can provide unsupervised direct delivery of professional services, including preventive, assessment, and therapeutic services" (*Resolution on the Master's Level Issue*, 1977). The APA position does not have unanimous support among the 102,101 psychological personnel referred to earlier, however.

Some psychological personnel possess "terminal master's degrees." Terminal master's degree training programs are usually designed to provide students with practical, specialized training in one or more of the applied areas of psychology. Often, students in these programs complete one or two years of course work combined with practicum ("hands-on") training in such areas as assessment, counseling, consultation, and organizational development. Many such programs also require a post-training field experience or internship. It is probably safe to say that two types of students are enrolled in terminal master's programs: those students who wish to work in applied settings and those who ultimately wish to pursue doctoral degrees but lack the necessary motivation or credentials to enter such programs immediately after completing their undergraduate work. Admission standards to terminal master's degree programs tend to be less competitive than admission requirements to doctoral-level programs (Ware, 1984).

Students interested in pursuing doctoral-level training have several decisions to make. Psychology students can pursue three kinds of doctoral degrees: the PhD, or Doctor of Philosophy, degree; the EdD, or Doctor of Education, degree; and the PsyD, or Doctor of Psychology, degree. The PhD is the traditional doctoral degree in many fields, including psychology. Most PhD training programs emphasize the "scientist-practitioner" model. That is, graduates of such programs are usually considered scientists first and practitioners second. Courses in research methodology and statistics are vital in preparing students to be active researchers wherever they are employed—in an applied setting or in university training programs. In addition, the completion of an empirically based doctoral dissertation is the necessary "exit" requirement in PhD programs.

The EdD degree is granted far more often by departments within colleges of education than by departments of psychology, which are traditionally within colleges of arts and sciences. Generally the research-related requirements for an EdD degree are not as rigorous as those for a PhD degree. Other requirements may also differ. It is not uncommon for school psychologists and counseling psychologists to receive EdD degrees.

The PsyD is relatively new within higher education. Students who wish to become doctoral-level practitioners rather than university trainers or researchers pursue the degree. PsyD programs are not always affiliated with universities—at times they are within separate entities known as schools of professional psychology.

Each of these degrees has advantages and disadvantages. Students interested in pursuing a graduate degree in psychology are well advised to consider their short-term and long-range career goals before making a choice. For example, if a student's goals involve working with children, adolescents, or adults in a direct service delivery setting, either a terminal master's degree or a PsyD degree may be the most appropriate level of training. Those wishing to teach college-level psychology and to conduct research, however, should seriously consider a PhD program. In addition to considering their goals, students must also consider such factors as the time, money, motivation, and ability necessary for graduate-level training.

Several authors have debated the merits of possessing a master's degree in psychology in gaining admission to doctoral-level training programs. D. P. Saccuzzo and R. H. Schulte (1978) examined the policies of PhD programs with respect to applicants with master's degrees. Their findings, reflecting 100 clinical programs and 59 nonclinical programs, indicate that possession of a master's degree either had no effect on a student's chance of acceptance or was detrimental—it actually decreased one's chance of acceptance in about 80 percent of the cases. On the other hand, professional schools of psychology (schools offering the PsyD degree), may be more apt to accept students with master's degrees and with professional experience (Scheirer, 1983). Some may even require such credentials as prerequisites. Once again, students are encouraged to examine their own professional goals before deciding between a master's-level program and a doctoral-level program.

Another important degree-related concern centers upon the controversial notion of licensure. **Licensure** of psychologists involves the restriction of the title "psychologist" to those individuals meeting particular criteria. To determine what these criteria should be and whether licensing should be limited to doctoral-level individuals, several questions must be addressed:

- What are the pros and cons of restricting the use of the title "psychologist" to doctoral-level individuals?

- Does restricting the use of the title "psychologist" to doctoral-level individuals guarantee a certain level of competence?

- Should different standards for degree levels exist in the regulation of psychological practice, depending on the setting (for example, private practice versus a supervised agency-related practice)?

- Can public needs for psychological services be met if licensing is limited to doctoral-level psychologists?

In their comprehensive book devoted to these issues, B. R. Fretz and D. H. Mills (1980) present the arguments for and against restricting and licensing psychological services to doctoral-trained individuals. On the positive side, licensing of psychologists may protect the public from untrained professionals. It may also define and upgrade professional standards and provide a sort of quality control.

Alternatively, there is little evidence to support the notion that doctoral-level practitioners are actually more competent than master's-level practitioners. Licensing may lead to a shortage of professional services, especially among the poor and in rural areas. In addition, Fretz and Mills mention that licensing legislation may reflect the same sort of "paternalism" inherent in requiring motorists to wear seat belts or motorcyclists to wear helmets. The assumption seems to be that consumers are not able to make intelligent choices on their own and that the government must make such decisions for them.

Within the four applied areas of psychology, what percentage of practitioners are master's level and what percentage are doctoral level? Again referring to the census of psychological personnel reported in 1985, the vast majority of clinical psychologists and industrial/organizational psychologists (approximately 78 percent of each) hold doctorate degrees. The majority of counseling psychologists (approximately 64 percent) are doctorate-level individuals as well.

On the other hand, only about one fourth of the school psychologists (24 percent) have doctorate degrees. In fact, individuals with master's degrees most often reported school psychology as their major field. Many school psychology programs offer the EdS, or Educational Specialist degree, requiring more training and experience than the master's degree but less than a doctoral-degree program.

The setting in which the psychologist works may play a critical role in determining the level of training needed. Psychologists working in supervised settings (schools, mental health centers, university counseling centers, or the personnel office of a large industry, for instance) may be qualified to carry out their professional duties with a master's degree in the relevant area of expertise. Individuals wishing to work in unsupervised settings, often called "private practice," are generally required to have doctoral-level training and to be licensed by the state in which they practice. Those who wish to teach psychology at the university level must usually possess the doctorate degree as well.

The issue of a minimum or entry-level degree has been a source of controversy for many years, and it is not likely to be resolved in the near future. Although individuals with terminal master's degrees from departments of psychology are not recognized as psychologists by the American Psychological Association, their numbers are large and increasing. J. Stapp, A. M. Tucker, and G. R. VandenBos (1985) indicate that between 1973 and 1983, graduate programs in psychology awarded 32,744 doctoral degrees and 84,000 master's degrees. Undoubtedly, many of those master's degree recipients will pursue doctorates. That will still leave a large number of people whose highest degree is a master's degree in psychology, many of whom will be employed by schools, industries, mental health centers, and so forth. The master's-doctoral degree controversy is far from settled.

Career Options in Applied Psychology

It is probably no surprise that psychology is a large field of study encompassing many subfields or specialty areas. In fact, the index of the 1984 edition of *Graduate Study in Psychology and Associated Fields*, a publication of the American Psychological Association, lists 121 individually identified fields of psychology. Altogether, prospective graduate students could choose from 3,265 programs in psychology. The ten areas with the greatest number of degree programs are listed in Table 2.1. Note that in this table no differentiation is made between master's and doctoral-training programs.

For this book I have chosen to discuss the four "traditional" areas of applied psychology—clinical psychology, counseling psychology, industrial/organizational psychology, and school psychology. Each of these areas is included in Table 2.1. Each one has its own division within the American Psychological Association, and each one has a unique relationship to psychological testing.

The remainder of this chapter provides brief descriptions of the four applied fields mentioned. I have addressed specific questions regarding the training, roles, and functions of individuals in each of the areas. In addition, Chapters 3 through 6 present the assessment-related roles and functions of

T A B L E 2.1 Psychology Areas with the Largest Number
of Graduate Programs

Area	Number of Graduate Programs
Clinical	239
Experimental-General	178
School	158
Social	127
General	117
Developmental	116
Industrial/Organizational	112
Cognitive	98
Counseling Psychology	85
Physiological	68

psychologists in the four fields. References at the conclusion of Chapters 3
through 6 offer readers the opportunity to learn more about the applied areas
of psychology.

Clinical Psychology

It is probably safe to say that when most people think of psychologists, the
image they conjure up is that of a clinical psychologist sitting in a chair saying
very little, while a patient on a couch rambles on about his or her life, loves, and
problems. This model has been popularized by novels, television series, and
films. Although the image contains certain elements of truth, the psychologist is
often portrayed as either overly incompetent—a "bungler"—or exaggeratedly
competent—a "miracle worker" who within moments identifies the patient's
"problem" and effects a cure.

Clinical psychologists usually possess PhD degrees from clinical psychology programs within departments of psychology at universities. Their graduate
training includes course work in research methodology, assessment techniques,
abnormal psychology, psychology of personality, and individual and group
psychotherapy. An important component of clinical psychology training programs is the time spent in practicum, or hands-on, training. In these experiences, future clinical psychologists go through a sort of apprenticeship under
the close and careful supervision of practicing psychologists. Gradually students are able to try out their newly acquired clinical skills with actual clients,
often in a university-based psychology clinic. Upon completing course and
practicum requirements, students in clinical psychology programs continue their
training with a yearlong clinical internship, again under supervision from clinical psychologists.

Often confusion exists as to the differences between clinical psychologists and psychiatrists. Psychiatrists complete three or four years of training in medical school. They take the same course work required of all physicians with little if any specific course work in psychology. The yearlong internship for the psychiatrist-to-be is similar if not identical to the internship for any other doctor. The psychiatrist is first and foremost a medical doctor; specialization in psychiatry develops during the three years of residency required for full membership in the American Psychiatric Association.

The clinical psychologist has extensive training in psychological theory and practice, including psychological testing, whereas the psychiatrist has general medical training with advanced training and practice in psychiatry. The psychologist is not licensed to authorize any type of medical treatment, particularly medication. But psychological testing calls for the psychologist's expertise. A recent article (Kingsbury, 1987) suggests that the distinctions between clinical psychologists and psychiatrists reflect fundamental differences in the ways in which the two professions view science, clinical cases, professional experience, and each other.

One reason for the confusion between the two professions undoubtedly stems from the fact that clinical psychology originally evolved from the long-established field of medicine and from the much more recent developments in the field of psychology. Much of clinical psychology's history reflects an acceptance of the "medical model." Within this model, the psychologist attempts to diagnose an individual's problem based on existing symptoms and to treat that problem until the patient is cured, just as a medical doctor attempts to diagnose, treat, and cure the symptoms of a physically ill patient.

The clinical psychologist diagnoses and treats individuals with a wide range of difficulties and disabilities. Clinical psychologists are employed in a variety of settings—Veterans Administration hospitals, university counseling centers, community mental health centers, and psychology clinics. Many spend some or all of their time in private practice. Others may be employed by prisons, industries, or the armed services. The roles and functions of clinical psychologists may be determined as much by their place of employment, as by their training, interests, and specialization.

An article entitled "Clinical Psychologists in the 1970s" (Garfield & Kurtz, 1976) describes the results of a survey of one third of the members in the American Psychological Association's Division 12, the Division of Clinical Psychology. Survey respondents were asked to estimate the percentage of time they spent in each of twelve designated activities. The results indicate that 25 percent of the clinicians' time was spent in individual psychotherapy, nearly 14 percent in teaching activities, and slightly more than 13 percent in administrative activities. Close to 10 percent of the respondents' time was spent in diagnosis and assessment activities. This, of course, does not mean that an individual clinical psychologist's time is divided up in this manner. Some of the psychologists polled undoubtedly spend a majority of their time in individual psychotherapy. Others, perhaps in university settings, spend most of their time teaching and conducting research while seeing few if any clients.

Counseling Psychology

Counseling psychologists provide a wide variety of psychological services in many settings—colleges and universities, hospitals, and industries, to name a few. As mentioned earlier, despite popular confusion between clinical psychologists and psychiatrists, there are some fairly clear-cut distinctions between the two professions in terms of course work, degree, and practical experience or training. Distinctions between clinical psychologists and counseling psychologists are not nearly so clear. In fact, in some settings counseling and clinical psychologists work together performing the same functions and seeing the same sorts of clients.

In most situations, however, there are ways in which clinical and counseling psychologists differ from each other. Much of the remainder of this section will attempt to explain those differences and to define counseling psychology as a profession in its own right. In her book *Fields of Applied Psychology*, Anne Anastasi (1979) provides a detailed and comprehensive discussion of the similarities and differences between clinical psychology and counseling psychology. Similarities include an emphasis on a warm, trusting, nonthreatening relationship between the psychologist and his or her client combined with a need for and dependence on verbal communication skills. Counseling and clinical psychologists may also be trained in and use some of the same therapeutic approaches (for example, client-centered or behavior modification–based therapy).

The differences between counseling psychology and clinical psychology as described by Anastasi are fairly clear in a theoretical sense. These distinctions may not be quite so clear in actual practice, however. Many of the differences can be traced to the history and development of the two areas. Counseling psychology has evolved from the vocational-guidance movement. Unlike clinical psychology, which is based on the medical model, counseling psychologists tend to be less concerned with searching for causes of difficulty and more concerned with present and future functioning. Whereas clinical psychologists emphasize the general weaknesses in personality functioning that need to be "cured," counseling psychologists emphasize an individual's strengths in attempting to work through a particular difficulty. Clinical psychologists try to change a client's personality structure, while counseling psychologists try to solve problems without making major changes.

Within this sort of framework it should be apparent that clinical psychologists often spend considerably more time with an individual client and use traditional psychotherapeutic techniques such as psychoanalysis far more frequently than do counseling psychologists. One reason for these differences in approach and duration of services may be the type of clients they see. Clinical psychologists tend to work with clients whose problems literally disable them and prevent them from living normal lives. Counseling psychologists tend to work with clients whose problems temporarily disrupt one or more aspects of their lives but who otherwise function adequately.

A comparative study of two surveys, one measuring practices of 479 clinical psychologists and the other measuring practices of 716 counseling psychologists, yields some data-based conclusions regarding the differences between the two specialty areas (Watkins, Lopez, Campbell, & Himmell, 1986). Almost two thirds of the clinical psychologists viewed themselves as primarily "clinical practitioners" compared to only about half of the counseling psychologists. But 28.5 percent of the counseling psychologists considered themselves primarily "academicians" compared to only 17.3 percent of the clinical psychologists. Such self-descriptions may be related to employment site and status.

In terms of their primary place of employment, clinical psychologists were employed most frequently in private practice (31.1 percent), next often in university settings, usually in departments of psychology (21.7 percent), and finally in hospitals (15 percent). Counseling psychologists were most often employed in university settings, usually not in departments of psychology (31.7 percent), and rarely in hospital settings (5.4 percent).

To muddle further the distinction between clinical psychology and counseling psychology, we must also mention the differences between counseling psychologists and counselors. These differences are not as obvious as we might hope. Counseling psychologists often feel that counseling programs are not as rigorous as counseling psychology programs (Asher & Asher, 1978; Foreman, 1977; Weigel, 1977) and that counselors may try to "pass themselves off" as counseling psychologists despite their less rigorous training. Unfortunately, few data-based studies are available to substantiate or refute these accusations.

One measurable difference between types of programs pertains to psychology course-hours required for admission to various programs (Holmes, Wurtz, & Waln, 1982). The Holmes et al. study found that even at the PhD level, nonpsychology-based counseling programs required a mean of only 0.48 (standard deviation = 1.16) psychology courses as prerequisites for admission. Doctoral level counseling psychology programs, on the other hand, required a mean of 6.0 psychology courses (standard deviation = 4.24) as a prerequisite for program admission. Thus, it seems that counseling psychology programs are more concerned that their students are well grounded in the fundamentals of psychology, at least prior to their entry into graduate programs.

Within counseling psychology there are many areas of specialization, including graduate programs that emphasize substance abuse counseling, marriage and family counseling, vocational counseling, college counseling, and so forth. Counseling psychologists are employed by colleges and universities, government agencies, prisons, community social service agencies, hospitals, and many other organizations. The type of training individuals receive, coupled with their employment setting and personal preferences, will to a large extent dictate their on-the-job roles and functions.

Industrial/Organizational Psychology

Industrial psychology and organizational psychology (I/O) started out as separate bodies of knowledge. By 1970, however, the two had merged sufficiently to require a name change for APA's Division 14 from the Division of Industrial Psychology to the Division of Industrial and Organizational Psychology. The roots of I/O psychology combine several fields of psychology, including clinical psychology, engineering psychology, measurement psychology, and social psychology. The field of I/O psychology today addresses human behavior as it applies to groups, organizations, and industries.

The industrial/organizational psychologist is interested in the behavior of individuals and groups within work settings. I/O psychologists may be concerned with any or all of the following questions:

- Who is the best person for a particular job?

- What skills or abilities does it take to be successful in a particular job?

- How can we match the right person to the right job?

- What aspects of behavior differentiate between competent and incompetent performance on the job?

- How can we educate individuals to be better (or more productive) employees?

- How can we improve employee morale?

- What can be done about those factors interfering with productivity (turnover rates, absenteeism, substance abuse, and so on.)?

- How can changes best be introduced into an organization?

- What characteristics or behaviors are important for supervisory personnel?

A recent survey of industrial/organizational psychologists reported by A. Howard (1982) reveals the following characteristics of the 2,800 APA members designating I/O psychology as their major field. The majority (74.9 percent) held PhD degrees, as opposed to 19.8 percent who held master's degrees. The remaining 5.3 percent held a variety of other degrees. Approximately half of the respondents had earned their degrees specifically in industrial/organizational psychology.

In terms of work setting, 32.8 percent were working in businesses and industries; 29.9 percent of the survey respondents were employed by colleges and universities; 14.5 percent worked in "professional settings of a non-mental-health nature"; 8.3 percent worked for government agencies; 6.5 percent were employed by mental health-related services; and 8.1 percent worked in "other settings."

When asked to select their own areas of specialization within I/O psychology, survey respondents most frequently chose general personnel and general management and organization. "Selection and placement" was the specific personnel-related specialty area mentioned most frequently, whereas "organizational behavior" was the specific management and organizational specialty mentioned most often.

Graduate training in industrial/organizational psychology usually includes work in a variety of psychology- and business-related course work. Within psychology such a program would most likely include work in statistics, research methodology, program evaluation, psychological assessment of individuals and groups (from a theoretical as well as an applied perspective), crisis intervention, stress management, group dynamics, and social psychology. Business courses might include personnel management, organizational development and behavior, legal and ethical issues, labor relations, and marketing.

As with all of the applied areas of psychology, oral and written communication skills and interpersonal sensitivity are vital. Computer skills have also become increasingly important. Additionally, an industrial/organizational psychologist employed by a large company would probably be expected to do some public speaking, conduct meetings, and play a part in some decision making.

School Psychology

Psychologists whose primary places of employment are public schools are called school psychologists. The professional roots of school psychology include the mental health movement, special education, and psychological testing, as well as the fields of clinical and counseling psychology. In addition, state and federal laws have had a major impact on the practice of school psychology.

The major functions for most school psychologists relate to the **child study** or **diagnostic model**. Within this model, a child who is experiencing some sort of problem—academic, behavioral, or emotional—is referred, usually by the classroom teacher, to the school psychologist to determine the reason for the difficulty. The psychologist in turn suggests a remedial plan that can be used within the classroom or assists in placing the child in a more appropriate educational environment (usually a special education class). The school psychologist uses several different methods or techniques to diagnose the problem and to suggest or prescribe remediations. Such an approach might include:

* Interviewing the child, the parents, and the teacher.

* Examining school records and results of any previous assessments.

* Observing the child in the natural environment, for example, classroom or playground.

* Selecting, administering, and scoring a battery of psycho-educational assessment instruments, including tests of cognitive development, academic achievement, perceptual-motor development, personality, and behavior.

- Formulating some hypotheses about the child's strengths and weaknesses.

- Developing a tentative remedial plan.

- Sharing the results of the assessment process orally at parent conferences and multidisciplinary staffings.

- Writing a report summarizing the assessment results.

- Helping to implement the remedial plan.

- Following up to determine the child's progress.

Although most school psychologists spend large amounts of time and effort engaged in these child study–related activities, the role of the school psychologist is by no means limited to these activities. Large amounts of the school psychologist's time may be spent in any or all of the following activities as well.

Consultation Loosely defined as a problem-solving process between professionals, consultation has many possibilities for school psychologists. Teachers may consult with the psychologist about discipline problems in their classrooms, introducing mental health topics into the school curriculum, or dealing with resistant parents. Increasingly, teachers may consult school psychologists to help them assist their students in coping with parental divorce, abuse, or other crisis situations. Consultation is considered an *indirect* role because the school psychologist does not work directly with the students but rather indirectly through the teachers. In a similar way, school psychologists may consult with school principals and other school personnel to provide indirect assistance on a variety of topics ranging from group testing to crisis intervention.

Individual or Group Counseling It is not unusual for a teacher or parent to refer a student to the school psychologist for a specific emotional, social, or behavioral difficulty. A lengthy test battery is not particularly relevant in these cases. For example, one child may be having difficulty adjusting to a parental divorce; another child may not know how to make friends; a third child may be acting aggressively during recess. Because school psychologists are often the only mental health specialists employed by school systems (especially within elementary school settings), such cases may be seen as appropriate referrals. Most school psychologists do have some training, experience, and interest in working with such children and will spend time clarifying the problem area and trying to help them understand and cope with the difficulty. Few school psychologists, however, have the time or the training needed for long-term psychotherapy. In cases demanding such therapy, school psychologists should familiarize themselves with counseling services in the community in order to offer appropriate referral information to these troubled youngsters and their parents. This networking function—linking children with available resources—is becoming an increasingly popular and important role for the psychologist in the schools.

In addition to short-term individual counseling, school psychologists may become involved in group counseling activities. Usually such activities have a particular focal point (for instance, enhancing cooperation skills and decreasing aggression in sixth-grade boys, helping third-grade girls develop higher self-esteem, and assisting a group of ten-to-twelve-year-olds cope with their parents' remarriages). Many school psychologists also work with groups of parents. Common topics might include a positive approach to discipline or coping with a disabled child.

Child study, consultation, and individual and group counseling are some of the more frequent activities engaging school psychologists. Depending on their skills, work settings, training, and interests, psychologists in the schools may also be involved in conducting research and in program development (for example, helping start a gifted program or developing inservice workshops for school personnel).

Subspecialties within Psychology: Shall We Each Hang Separately?

This chapter is devoted to describing the four traditional applied areas of psychology. It has shown that many of the distinctions between two or more of the fields are clearer in theory than in practice. As we describe the assessment-related functions of each of the applied areas within the next four chapters, you will find that the major differences in test usage—especially between clinical, counseling, and school psychologists, the so-called "human service" branches of psychology—seem to rest more with the client's make-up than with the psychologist's particular area of specialization.

The notion that the clinical psychologist follows the medical model whereas the counseling psychologist follows the vocational guidance model sounds reasonable, at least on paper. When a clinical psychologist and a counseling psychologist work next door to each other at the same agency, or are in the same group of private-practice associates, then such theoretical differences may all but disappear.

R. E. Fox, A. L. Kovacs, and S. R. Graham have suggested (1985) that we do away with individual areas of specialization within psychology and concentrate instead on a united "human services delivery model." I doubt that such a move will ever take place, and I am not completely convinced that it would be beneficial or even appropriate. The idea of unity, however, is certainly thought-provoking and tempting in light of the time and energy professionals in the applied areas spend in vigorous debates.

IDEAS FOR FURTHER STUDY

1. Look at the most recent edition of *Graduate Study in Psychology & Associated Fields.* For each of the four areas (clinical, counseling, industrial/organizational, and school), compare the number of master's programs to the number of doctoral programs.

2. What are the current regulations in your state regarding licensure or registration of psychologists? You can write to the Psychologist Licensing Board in your state's capital for this information.

3. Check the Yellow Pages of several telephone directories for advertised psychological services. Look under psychologists, physicians, psychiatry, counselors, and therapists. What information is presented to help the consumer who needs such services? Call and ask what services are available. Are there clinics or mental health centers in your area that provide the same services? Again, call and ask what services are available.

4. Does insurance cover expenses incurred during therapy?

5. Does your state have rules or regulations protecting the information shared by a client during therapy? If so, are there any exceptions? Write to the Psychologist Licensing Board in your state's capital for this information.

6. For psychologists employed by school districts, courts, or businesses and industries, the question "Who is the client?" is often voiced. Is it the person receiving your professional services or the person paying you for your services? Choose one of the four fields and discuss the "Who is the client?" question within that field. Then answer the question "What difference does it make how the psychologist defines the client?"

• • • • •
• • • • •
• • • • •
• • • • •

C H A P T E R   3

Psychological Assessment and the Clinical Psychologist

Clinical psychologists work in a wide variety of settings with clients of every age and with every type of presenting problem. The roles and functions of any individual clinical psychologist are largely determined by a combination of training, employment setting, and personal preference. Certainly the approaches to and applications of assessment techniques vary from one clinical psychologist to the next.

Some general statements about the assessment practices of clinical psychologists have been reported in the literature. For example, a study by T. C. Wade and T. B. Baker (1977) examined test-usage practices and opinions about tests among a sample of members of Division 12 (Clinical Psychology) of the American Psychological Association. Across a variety of settings, the clinicians sampled spent more than one third of their time administering and evaluating objective and projective psychological tests. The "therapeutic orientation" (Freudian, behavior therapy, and so forth) did not seem to have an impact on the assessment practices of the clinicians. In terms of the purposes of test administration, Wade and Baker found that nearly half (47.4 percent) used test results to aid in diagnoses; 16.2 percent used tests in determining the appropriate treatment for a client; and one fourth (24.7 percent) used test results for both diagnoses and treatment assignment. The psychologists in the survey indicated that in making decisions about diagnoses and treatment, they used test results in combination with their own clinical judgment.

Two recent articles (Lubin, Larsen, Matarazzo, & Seever, 1986a; 1986b) compared clinical psychologists' assessment practices across seven different employment settings: private practice, military settings, psychiatric hospitals, community clinics and mental health centers, counseling centers, centers for developmental disabilities and mental retardation, and VA medical centers. A 10-percent sample of clinical psychologists in each of the settings received a questionnaire regarding their assessment practices. As might be expected, there were some large differences in specific assessment instruments, and assessment practices varied according to the setting. For example, although the Minnesota Multiphasic Personality Inventory (MMPI) was ranked first, second, or third for frequency of usage by psychologists in six of the seven settings, it was ranked eleventh for psychologists in centers for the developmentally disabled. Similarly, the Wechsler Adult Intelligence Scale (WAIS) was ranked first or second by everyone except the psychologists in counseling centers, by whom it was ranked ninth.

Any number of variables may account for these differences:

- The age and general ability level of the clientele in each setting.

- The training and theoretical orientation of clinical psychologists who choose to work in particular settings.

- The general "mission," or reason for being, of each setting.

The following examples may help illustrate the diverse applications of assessment techniques based on settings.

The Clinical Psychologist in Private Practice

The clinical psychologist who decides to pursue the private practice of psychology may do so for several reasons. First, private practice is usually considered the most lucrative form of practicing psychology. It is the one setting where psychologists work "on commission" rather than for a salary. Second, private practice offers the clinical psychologist the advantage of autonomy. No one supervises the private practitioner. There are no agency guidelines that dictate the number and types of clients that psychologists must see each year. Additionally, there is usually less red tape associated with private practice. For example, there would be no agency-mandated reports to complete, team meetings to attend, or other policies demanding compliance. Finally, some clinical psychologists are able to fit a part-time private practice schedule into their spare hours from teaching at a university or working at another job. Such an arrangement allows them to earn extra income while keeping their applied skills up to date.

On the other hand, full-time private practitioners do not have the security of a regular salary, whereas they incur overhead expenses that psychologists in agencies do not. At the very least, they must rent office space and buy office furniture and equipment, including test instruments, which can be quite costly. To help defray these costs many private practitioners work in groups—

sharing an office and secretarial services. In group settings psychologists can enjoy the financial benefits of private practice while sharing the expenses. In addition, although there is no supervisor to satisfy, there are colleagues nearby to turn to for advice in difficult cases and for empathy when crises or frustrations occur. Of course, even psychologists do not always get along with one another, and group practice settings may produce more problems than they solve.

Assuming that there are sufficient clients to pay their bills, private practitioners may wish to specialize in working with a specific client group—either of a particular age or with a specific presenting problem. One psychologist might choose to work with women; a second, with children; a third, with couples having marital difficulties, and a fourth, with elderly or disabled individuals. In other settings, such as community mental health centers, each psychologist might be expected to provide services for all types of clients. Specialization is a luxury that many agencies simply cannot afford; many psychologists in fact prefer the variety involved in the so-called generalist role.

The opportunity to specialize is not always available even to the private practitioner. A clinical psychologist in private practice in a rural area, for example, may feel a financial as well as a professional obligation to provide the whole range of psychological services to all members of the community. In addition, a small number of individuals may experience a particular problem, and the availability of mental health–related options may be even more limited.

In terms of assessment, depending on private practitioners' specialization, training, personal preferences, and the population they serve, psychologists might assess every client or never administer another test.

Dr. R. is a clinical psychologist engaged in private practice in a rural area with a population of approximately 30,000. The only other local mental health services are a community mental health center that has an extensive waiting list for its services and a school psychologist who provides services for the district's 7,000 children and adolescents (and has a tremendous backlog of referrals for her services). Last week, Dr. R. worked with the following clients :

- A four-year-old girl whose parents requested testing to determine whether their daughter meets the eligibility requirements for early admission to kindergarten.

- A couple seeking counseling as a "last-ditch" effort to save their marriage.

- An eight-year-old boy who has been labeled "behavior-disordered" by the local school psychologist and whose parents want a second opinion. (The school psychologist also strongly recommended family therapy, and the parents want to explore that possibility as well.)

- A sixteen-year-old boy who has dropped out of school and whose parents are concerned about his future.

In addition, Dr. R. gave a talk to the local Parent-Teacher Association about alcohol and drug abuse among teenagers. He consulted with the school psychologist and several school administrators about children's reactions to their parents' unemployment. Finally, he testified in court in a child custody case concerning a child he had been counseling.

How much of Dr. R.'s time was devoted to psychological testing and other phases of the assessment process? In the first example, Dr. R. administered several tests to the four-year-old girl. Throughout the testing he observed her behavior, her coordination, her manner of responding to questions, her abiliy to cope with frustration and failure, and so forth.

Based on the results of this total assessment process, Dr. R.'s comments to the parents may be summarized as follows:

You have a very smart little girl. Mandy scored in the bright-normal to gifted range on all of the tests I administered. In terms of whether she is ready for kindergarten, however, my best judgment is to wait the extra year. Mandy had to be tested in very brief intervals with frequent breaks—her ability to sit still for long periods of time is limited even in the one-to-one setting in which we worked. Mandy also seemed not to tolerate frustration very well. When there were two or three questions in a row that she could not answer, she either pouted or tried to change the subject and talk about something unrelated. Toward the end of our session, Mandy displayed very impulsive behavior. She would tell me the first thing that came into her mind rather than thinking the answer through thoroughly. Finally, Mandy's fine and gross motor coordination are not as well developed as her verbal abilities. I would recommend that you wait a year before you enroll Mandy in kindergarten. In the meantime, you might consider having her attend a preschool or enrolling her in a class at the YMCA in something like swimming or gymnastics. I just don't think she's ready for kindergarten yet.

Dr. R. did not use any psychological tests with the couple seeking marriage counseling. His informal appraisal of them was that both spouses were able to verbalize their concerns and frustrations well enough not to need any surveys for the time being.

Dr. R. did use several assessment techniques with Lonny, the eight-year-old boy who had been labeled "behavior-disordered" by the school psychologist. "Behavior-disordered" is a label used to describe children whose behavior within a classroom interferes with their own or their classmates' academic progress. Dr. R. observed Lonny in the classroom and at home, spoke at length to Lonny's teacher and parents, interviewed Lonny about his perceptions of the problems, and administered the Wechsler Intelligence Scale for Children—Revised (WISC-R) and the Peabody Individual Achievement Test (PIAT). Dr. R. also asked Lonny's teacher and parents to complete independent behavior checklists. Based on the results of all of these efforts, Dr. R. concurred with the school psychologist that Lonny did indeed qualify for the school's behavior-disordered services. A portion of his report read as follows:

Although Lonny scored within the average range of intelligence and academic achievement, he seems to have a great deal of difficulty relating to others— children as well as adults. He sees himself as the innocent victim ("other kids are always picking on me" and "my parents are always getting after me" are familiar comments), but this was not substantiated by any of the assessment data collected. Based on the behavior checklists completed by Lonny's teacher and parents and this examiner's observations of and interactions with Lonny, it appears that Lonny needs to work on the following behaviors:

1. *Assuming responsibility for his actions.*

2. *Learning alternative ways of relating to his peers.*

3. *Controlling his temper.*

4. *Learning to accept constructive criticism.*

5. *Improving his feelings of self-worth.*

6. *Conforming to basic rules at home and at school.*

Dr. R. and Lonny's family decided to begin family therapy as soon as possible. The local school psychologist agreed to act as a liaison between the school and Dr. R. to keep both sides aware of Lonny's progress and problems.

In Dr. R.'s first meeting with Fred, the sixteen-year-old who had dropped out of school, they discussed the reasons for Fred's decision and what had happened since. Fred was bored with school and he wanted to earn some money to help his recently unemployed parents. He found a job quickly at a fast-food place, but after a couple of weeks spent learning the job requirements, he discovered that work was "even more boring than school."

Dr. R. found Fred to be a very verbal and earnest young man who read a great deal. He suggested that he would like to administer the Wechsler Adult Intelligence Scale—Revised (WAIS-R). Fred quickly agreed. On the WAIS-R Fred scored in the gifted range, with an overall IQ of 142. He performed extremely well on all of the subtests and seemed to thoroughly enjoy the testing, especially the more challenging portions.

After explaining the results of the WAIS-R to Fred, Dr. R. urged him to seek vocational counseling at the community mental health center. Fred followed through on this suggestion and after completing the Strong-Campbell Interest Inventory (SCII) and discussing his scores with a counselor, he decided to give serious consideration to three occupations: lawyer, librarian, and reporter. Fred returned to Dr. R. and together they worked out the following plan for Fred:

1. Find out what to do to qualify for the High School Equivalency Exam (GED).

2. Enroll in a community creative writing class offered one night per week.

3. Apply at the local newspaper to see if any jobs are open.

Fred would check back with Dr. R. in one month.

Out of these four cases, Dr. R. used some type of formal assessment procedures with three and recommended outside (vocational assessment) testing with one. Dr. R.'s test results helped to answer some questions and yielded some useful information. Although Dr. R. is just one psychologist in private practice in a rural setting, it is probably clear that he works with a wide variety of clients and does not specialize in one type of case.

Dr. S., on the other hand, is a private practitioner in an upper middle-class suburban area who specializes in child custody cases. Dr. S. uses many formal and informal assessment techniques to gain as much information as possible about each child in a relatively short time. In child custody cases the referral questions are typically "What advantages could each parent provide if A. were to live with him or her?" "What disadvantages would relate to A.'s residing with each parent?" and "Is shared custody a viable alternative?"

In order to address these questions, Dr. S. administers a measure of general intellectual ability to the children and several personality measures to the children and their parents. Using the information from these tests coupled with data collected from extensive interviews with the parents and the children and from observations of the family members' interactions, Dr. S. might draw the following conclusion:

On the Wechsler Intelligence Scale for Children—Revised (WISC-R), Alice (who is ten years and six months old) scored within the bright-normal range (110–120) on the verbal scale, the performance scale, and the full-scale IQ score. Her responses to all types of questions indicate good reading skills and slightly above average language usage. These test results were in agreement with Alice's classroom teacher's observations.

Alice's behavior during the administration of the WISC-R seemed relaxed yet interested. She appeared to be paying attention to all of the questions, and she especially seemed to enjoy the performance items, such as Block Design and Object Assembly.

Following the WISC-R, Alice completed a personality assessment technique known as a Sentence Completion test. Alice seemed to feel comfortable talking to the examiner and was quite open in her responses. Her responses to the Sentence Completion test provided much additional information. When asked about school, Alice said she enjoys reading and arithmetic. She said she has several close friends at school and volunteered that "their parents are divorced too." Alice admitted that this year has been hard for her because "it seems strange not having my dad at home to talk to." When asked what she and her dad liked to do together, she said "take walks and play Scrabble."

When asked what she thought the best custody arrangement would be, Alice's answer seemed to be well thought out. "I guess I'll stay with my mom during the week and with my dad on weekends. That way, I'll have a lot of time with both of them, and I can still stay in the same school as my friends."

Alice's mother is a pleasant woman who described herself as a person who tries to make the best of a bad situation. She seems to be coping with her new "single-parent" status in a practical and responsible manner and has adjusted her schedule as much as possible to meet Alice's needs.

Alice's father is also a pleasant and hardworking person. Although he stated that he would prefer that Alice live with him, he admitted in the course of our discussions that he travels a great deal for his job, and he would have to make "some kind of arrangements" for Alice on those occasions.

Based upon all of the formal and informal assessment data, Alice seems to be adjusting well to her parents' separation. She seems to enjoy spending time with both parents and feels that she can continue to do that best if she lives with her mother during the week and her father on weekends. I would recommend this as the best solution at this time.

Clinical psychologists who work with families as a whole or with couples experiencing marital problems may rely far more heavily than Dr. S. does on informal assessments of clinical sessions (what is said to whom in what way?) and on nontraditional techniques than on standardized tests. The presenting problems usually render tests measuring aptitude, achievement, and visual motor abilities inappropriate.

Two examples of nontraditional assessment techniques that might be useful in family therapy are **Family Portraits** and **Family Sculptures.** In the Family Portrait Technique, the members of the family are given a large piece of paper and markers or crayons. The family is instructed (as a group) to draw a picture of their house. On completion of that drawing, the family members must put themselves in the picture. The family's drawing and the clinician's observations of the family's interactions while completing the drawing make the Family Portrait Technique a valuable assessment tool.

The technique known as Family Sculpting as described in C. E. Schaefer, J. M. Briesmeister, and M. E. Fitton (1984) is an assessment tool that examines family relationships through nonverbal behaviors. The members of a family in therapy are asked to "pose like statues to express a particular feeling or behavior." By observing the poses of the family members individually and collectively, the psychologist can examine alliances, rifts, and distances between family members.

Often, just the way in which family members position themselves during therapy sessions can provide the experienced clinician with clues about relationships within the family unit. For example, if the mother and son sit together while the father sits at the opposite end of the therapy room, the clinician may suspect that this is representative of the family's typical communication patterns. Of course, such clues need to be substantiated through additional observations.

The verbal fluency of the clients—how easily they can talk about their problems—may be critical in determining the need for various types of personality inventories. For example, if a couple comes in for counseling and the husband sits back looking disgusted with his arms crossed while his wife talks on and on about "their" problems, the psychologist will probably make a special effort to include the husband in the conversation. If the psychologist's best efforts to draw out the husband do not work, she may have both spouses complete the Marital Satisfaction Index. This assessment device serves two purposes. First, it engages the husband and the wife in examining various dimensions of their marriage. Second, it provides a catalyst—something specific the psychologist can use to get the husband to start talking.

Table 3.1 illustrates the relative frequencies of specific psychological assessment instruments used by clinical psychologists in private practice (Lubin et al., 1986b). Interestingly, nearly half of the psychologists in private practice in the Lubin et al. study reported that their assessment-related activities have decreased over the past ten years, whereas one third reported that their assessment-related activities have increased. What factors may account for these changes? Some possibilities include changes within the field of psychology, changes in the types of other services available, and social, legal, and economic changes.

Nearly three fourths of the private practitioners conducted assessments with fewer than 100 clients per year. Many of the clients who were tested were

T A B L E 3.1 Ranking of Usage of Ten Psychological Tests by Clinical Psychologists in Three Settings

	Rank in Setting		
Name of Test	Private Practice	CMHC	VA Medical Centers
Minnesota Multiphasic Personality Inventory	3	1	1.0
Wechsler Adult Intelligence Scale (and Revised)	1	2	2.0
Visual Motor Test (Bender-Gestalt)	2	3	3.0
Rorschach	4	5	8.5
Wechsler Intelligence Scale for Children (and Revised)	5	4	21.5
Sentence Completion (all kinds)	9	7	6.5
Thematic Apperception Test	7	8	10.5
Draw-A-Person Test	6	6	10.5
Rotter Sentence Completion Test	10	10	8.5
House-Tree-Person Test	8	9	15.0

From Lubin, Larsen, Matarazzo, & Seever, 1986a, 1968b.

referred for assessment by physicians in general (psychiatrists specifically), social workers, the courts, and other psychologists. Slightly more than half of the private practitioners used some sort of routine test battery in their assessments.

The Clinical Psychologist in the Community Mental Health Center

Psychological personnel at the master's and doctoral levels of training are often employed by community mental health centers. Prior to the development of such centers (in the 1960s and 1970s), individuals suffering from a wide range of psychological disorders faced limited treatment options. They could be hospitalized, they could undergo costly psychotherapy, or they could remain untreated. In 1963, Public Law 88-164 was enacted by the federal government to meet the "mental health" needs of the public. The legislation provided monies for the development of strategically located community mental health centers offering a wide range of preventive and treatment services. The reasons for the establishment of such centers were many and varied. Some of the major catalysts behind the passage of Public Law 88-164 included:

- *Saving money in the long run.* Money spent to prevent mental illness or to stop existing problems from becoming too severe (through early identification and intervention) could cut back on money spent for long-term care facilities.

- *Providing services to more people than were being served by existing institutions.* The "mental" hospitals were filled to capacity and yet were in no way able to meet all the mental health needs of the population.

- *Providing services to previously underserved or unserved populations.* Even though impoverished living conditions and the accompanying feelings of hopelessness may have increased the incidence of certain psychological disturbances, the poor were often the last people to receive treatment.

- *Providing better services based on improved concepts of treatment.* As psychological research methods advanced, it became increasingly clear that many individuals receiving inpatient treatment (hospitalization) were "getting better" until they were released and sent back to the environments that had first contributed to their problems. It became quite clear that removing people from their home environments to treat their problems might not always be the most sensible approach except in the most severe cases (for example, individuals posing some threat to themselves or others).

Overall, conditions were ripe for treatment centers that could:

- Work with a large number of people on an outpatient basis.

- Offer the advantage of being located within the community.

- Provide a variety of preventive activities.

- Act as a screening mechanism to help determine when an individual needs hospitalization.

Community mental health centers (CMHCs) were therefore established and continue to thrive. As with any institution, such centers vary in terms of services, employees, and staff orientation. Most, if not all, CMHCs have sliding fee scales—clients pay a graduated fee according to family size and income for the services they receive.

Clinical psychologists, community psychologists,* and counseling psychologists may all be employed by CMHCs. Certainly, there may be differences as well as similarities in the kinds of services offered by individuals trained in each of these areas of specialization. Counseling psychologists may be more involved in working with clients interested in vocational and educational planning. They may also work with groups (for example, clients interested in developing assertiveness skills or "displaced homemakers" who are not certain what to do next). Community psychologists in CMHCs may coordinate community outreach and prevention activities. Such activities attempt to "reach out" to people not currently served by the center in an effort to meet community needs and to prevent future problems. In order to fulfill this role adequately, CMHC psychologists would assess the community's needs for mental health services and would then develop a variety of programs and services to meet these needs.

The clinical psychologist in the community mental health center would most likely see the more disturbed clients at the center. He or she would tend to be responsible for the majority of assessment activities carried on within the CMHC (other than the vocational-type testing, which would likely be conducted by counseling psychologists). Table 3.1 shows the frequency of test usage by clinical psychologists in CMHCs, in private practice, and in VA medical centers (Lubin, Larsen, Matarazzo, & Seever, 1986a & 1986b). The fact that the Wechsler Adult Intelligence Scale (for persons sixteen and older) and the Wechsler Intelligence Scale for Children (for persons six through sixteen) are both among the top four tests given illustrates the wide range of ages with which psychologists in CMHCs work. Another study by Lubin et al. (1986a) indicates that compared to clinical psychologists in four other settings (psychiatric hospitals, counseling centers, centers for the developmentally disabled, and Veterans Administration medical centers), clinical psychologists employed by CMHCs see the fewest number of patients for psychological assessment per year. The median number of assessments conducted by clinical psychologists in CMHCs ranges from 51 to 100 per year, whereas the median percentage of assessments conducted by clinical psychologists in each of the other four settings is 101 to 500 per year.

_____

*Community psychology as a specialty area was an outgrowth of the legislation to develop CMHCs. For those interested in more information about community psychology, a list of references is provided at the end of this chapter.

According to Lubin et al. (1986a), two thirds of the assessments conducted by clinical psychologists in CMHCs are requested either by psychiatrists or by social workers.

One particularly interesting finding of the Lubin et al. (1986a) study is that 49 percent of the clinical psychologists in CMHCs in the study reported spending less time in assessment activities than they did ten years earlier. Why this is so is not completely clear. Certainly a major factor is that funding has decreased and that psychologists devote more time to providing direct services (that is, therapy) to the clients with the most serious difficulties. Many of these clients have already been assessed. In addition, there is little need for extensive assessment when programs or services are unavailable. Testing may also have declined because clinical psychologists in CMHCs have become more involved in preventive and outreach activities. A final possibility involves referrals for assessment. Two thirds of CMHC assessments are conducted at the request of psychiatrists and social workers; the decline in assessments would seem to indicate that these requests are fewer in number.

In a large CMHC, the staff may include several psychologists with a variety of interests and areas of expertise. Like private practitioners, clinical psychologists in CMHCs may specialize in particular types of cases. Although a clinical psychologist at such a center may see a wide variety of clients, one clinical psychologist may nonetheless specialize in substance abuse cases, another in neuropsychological assessments, and a third in cases involving children. When referrals are made to the CMHC, and when scheduling and other constraints allow, the center attempts to match a client with a particular problem with the psychologist specializing in that area. If such scheduling is not possible, the psychologist to whom the client is assigned may consult with the "specialist" regarding particular details of the case.

The amount of time the clinical psychologist in a CMHC devotes to assessment-related activities is dictated by the types of clients and the psychologist's training and personal preferences. In addition, the policies of the CMHC's administrative staff and the demographic variables and needs of the community may have an impact on assessment practices. Whenever psychological testing is an option, regardless of the setting, administrators must make an informal estimate of the benefits derived versus the costs incurred. Testing takes time and money in terms of staff hours, purchasing and replenishing test supplies, and so forth. If a community mental health center is faced with a tremendous backlog of cases, administrators and staff may suggest that under ordinary circumstances psychological testing should be a low-priority activity. In such cases, the underlying assumption is that the benefits of testing (for example, better understanding of the client and more quantifiable information) are not strong enough to outweigh the costs of staff time.

In other instances, a CMHC may receive a large number of referrals from individuals undergoing acute reactions to a wide variety of crises. The media overwhelm us with stories of violent crimes—child abuse, kidnapping, rape, robbery, and hostage taking, to name a few. Many of the victims of these crimes need the help of mental health professionals immediately. Subjecting these individuals to lengthy assessment batteries prior to the provision of short- or long-term therapeutic services would be absurd and probably counterproductive.

The following examples suggest the types of people with whom a clinical psychologist in a community mental health center might work. Dr. C. is currently seeing the following clients:

- A group of area farm families who requested counseling to help them cope with the recent suicide of one of their friends and neighbors.

- A recovering alcoholic and his family who are having difficulties adjusting to the changes brought about by the father's "new (sober) personality."

- A thirteen-year-old girl who has been sexually abused by her mother's boyfriend.

- A recently divorced forty-year-old woman who is having difficulty dealing with all of the changes in her life.

Dr. C. is also working with the local hospital to treat substance abusers and is the consultant to a shelter for battered women.

How much of Dr. C.'s week is devoted to assessment procedures? In the case of the farm families coping with their neighbor's suicide, Dr. C. did not see any reason to use psychological testing or assessment. Instead, she employed crisis intervention techniques to help deal with the families' reactions.

Dr. C. did not use any formal assessment techniques in her work with the recovering alcoholic and his family. In this case she used some of the informal family therapy assessment techniques described earlier in this chapter to help her understand the communication patterns and particularly sensitive issues within the family unit.

With Sheila, the thirteen-year-old sexual abuse victim, Dr. C. used some personality assessment techniques. Sheila was rather quiet and did not volunteer much information in the initial interview. Dr. C. hoped that she might find it easier, at least initially, to communicate her thoughts and feelings through assessment techniques such as drawings or forced-choice personality measures requiring her merely to select the most appropriate response. Based on Sheila's drawings of her family and her answers to the Mooney Problem Checklist, Dr. C. decided to focus on Sheila's self-esteem, her relationship with her mother, and her attitude toward dating and sexuality. Dr. C. and Sheila agreed that Sheila's mother should attend several sessions so that they could begin to deal with Sheila's anger and lack of trust and her mother's apparent feelings of guilt.

Dr. C. did not employ any formal assessment procedures with the recently divorced woman. She did recommend, however, that the client, Roberta, undergo a battery of vocational aptitude tests to determine the most appropriate employment possibilities for her to pursue.

Of these four cases, Dr. C. administered psychological tests to only one client. One additional client was referred for testing to the counseling psychologist in charge of vocational assessment.

The Clinical Psychologist in a Veterans Administration Medical Center

It may astound you to learn that close to 1,300 psychologists are employed by the Veterans Administration (VA), making it "the largest single employer of psychologists in the free world" (Cranston, 1986; p. 990). The VA medical center system provides a wide variety of health-related services to veterans. Some of these veterans suffer from physical injuries incurred during active combat. Others suffer from psychological injuries incurred as a direct result of combat. Still others suffer from a combination of physical and psychological combat-related injuries. Symptoms of these injuries may manifest themselves during combat or may lie dormant, only to appear many years later.

Clinical and counseling psychologists provide a wide variety of psychological services to veterans in VA medical centers. A recent article listed some of the types of VA programs and services involving psychologists (West & Lips, 1986):

Mental health treatment programs

Day treatment programs

Day hospitals

Day dependence treatment centers

Alcohol rehabilitation units

Programs for Vietnam veterans (including outreach)

In some ways the services are similar to those offered by a CMHC. A VA medical center, however, serves a much more homogeneous population. Clinical psychologists in VA medical centers tend to work primarily with adult males—no children and few adolescents. In addition, at the time of their induction into the armed services, recruits undergo physical examinations. Patients in VA hospitals are therefore rarely victims of chronic, congenital illnesses. On the other hand, often as a direct or indirect consequence of combat experience, psychologists in VA hospitals may treat many individuals with alcohol or drug dependencies.

Nearly half of the psychologists employed in VA medical centers reported doing more assessment than they did ten years ago (Lubin, et al., 1986a). VA center psychologists have a far greater caseload than psychologists employed by a CMHC. Only 2 percent of psychologists in CMHCs reported working with more than 500 clients during the year prior to the Lubin et al. (1986a) survey. Compare that with the 36 percent of psychologists in VA centers who work with more than 500 clients (Lubin et al., 1986a). In fact, 17 percent of psychologists in VA medical centers worked with more than 1,000 clients or patients in the year prior to the Lubin et al. (1986a) survey. A psychologist working 250 days per year (five days per week with two weeks of vacation) would have to see a minimum of four new clients each day to meet such a quota.

Of the seven settings for clinical psychologists reported by Lubin et al. (1986a & b), psychologists in VA medical centers were the least likely to use a routine test battery in their work. Nearly three fourths (71 percent) of the assessments conducted by psychologists at VA centers are the result of referrals from psychiatrists. The psychologist in these cases completes the assessment techniques most pertinent to the specific referral questions. The patient, his family, and other members of the health services team may all share in test results. In the VA system, as in other large organizations, the psychologist may have specific functions as a member of a team of professionals.

Certainly, many of the assessment-related functions of a clinical psychologist in a VA medical center are similar to those of other clinical psychologists. For illustrative purposes, however, let us look at the caseload of Dr. V., a clinical psychologist who has been employed for five years by a large urban VA medical center. Over the course of these five years, Dr. V. has become increasingly interested in **neuropsychological assessment**. Simply stated, neuropsychology attempts to examine the relationships between the brain and behavior. Neuropsychological assessment measures an individual's ability to perform a variety of activities and allows the psychologist to make inferences about the possible presence of brain damage. Because of the unique client population in VA medical centers, neuropsychology is a particularly appropriate specialization for clinical psychologists employed in these centers. Many of the patients referred to Dr. V. have a combination of physical and psychological symptoms attributable at least in part to such factors as combat-related experiences, substance abuse, or aging. Often, physicians at the medical center refer patients to Dr. V. for neuropsychological assessments after extensive medical testing.

A comprehensive neuropsychological examination depends on a wide variety of information sources. The following discussion presents some of these sources and how they might be incorporated into Dr. V.'s assessments. As with all psychological assessments, these sources vary according to the presenting problem, age, and approximate ability level of the individual as well as the availability of informed others within the client's environment. Issues of professional ethics, such as confidentiality, are just as essential in a neuropsychological assessment as in any other form of psychological assessment.

Neuropsychological assessment attempts to ascertain an individual's personality characteristics, abilities, strengths, and weaknesses, and, when applicable, to examine behavior that may have changed as a result of an event or events (for example, a blow to the head or a seizure). In order to gather this information in an organized manner, Dr. V. often begins an examination by asking the client some or all of the following questions. Of course, there are situations in which clients are unable to answer the questions themselves. In those cases, Dr. V. might question a close family member, caretaker, or friend.

Current Functioning and Background Information

1. What is the problem?

2. How long has this been going on?

3. What made you decide to seek treatment now?

4. Has the problem stayed the same or gotten worse?

5. Is the problem always with you or does it come and go?

6. If it comes and goes, have you noticed any pattern or sequence?

7. Have you noticed any difficulties with:
   a. attention and concentration?
   b. remembering?
   c. ability to read and write?
   d. orientation—getting from one familiar place to another?
   e. regular habits—cooking, driving, and so on?

8. Have you had any difficulty with:
   a. sleeping?
   b. falling asleep?
   c. nightmares?
   d. restless sleep?

9. Have your eating habits changed? Has your appetite decreased or increased? Have you experienced any food cravings?

10. Are you taking any medication?

11. How much alcohol do you consume?

12. Are you taking or have you taken any other types of drugs? For how long? What dosages?

While Dr. V. is conducting this interview with the client, he is also observing the behavior of the client, with respect to:

Verbal ability

Facial expression

Quickness of response

Thoughtfulness of responses

Affect, or emotional state

Activity level

Following the interview, Dr. V. might also gather the following information.

Background Information

From family members or others:

1. Have you noticed any changes in his behavior?

2. When did these changes occur?

3. How frequently does he act this way?

4. What was he like before?

5. Have there been any recent major changes in his life (for example, divorce, illness)?

Complete Health History

From the client, previous medical reports, and family members, Dr. V. attempts to gather information regarding:

1. Developmental history:

Was the birth normal?

Any complications during pregnancy or childbirth?

Did he grow normally (height and weight)?

2. Developmental milestones:

Did he walk and talk at "normal" ages?

Did he seem particularly delayed or advanced in any area?

3. General health:

Any major illnesses or accidents?

Any chronic conditions for which he is currently being treated?

4. Family health history:

Are parents still living? If so, ages? Parents' general health and functioning? If deceased, at what age and from what cause?

Siblings?

Children?

Grandparents?

Is the client currently taking any medication?

Does the client have any history of substance abuse?

Neuropsychological Test Batteries

Following the referral procedures, the initial interview, and the examination of any relevant records and reports, Dr. V. may administer a test battery in order to observe the client's reactions to a variety of tasks. The two best known and most widely used neuropsychological test batteries are the **Halstead-Reitan Neuropsychological Test Battery** and the **Luria-Nebraska Neuropsychological Battery.**

The Halstead-Reitan Battery is made up of five tests or categories of behavior:

1. Input measures.

2. Measures of verbal abilities.

3. Measures of spatial, sequential, and manipulatory abilities.

4. Measures of reasoning, abstract thinking, and concept formation.

5. Output measures.

The Luria-Nebraska Neuropsychological Battery (LNNB) is made up of 269 items which were developed to measure an individual's level of functioning on the following eleven clinical scales:

Motor

Rhythm

Tactile

Visual

Receptive Speech

Expressive Speech

Writing

Reading

Arithmetic

Memory

Intellectualization Process (Intelligence)

Based on the individual's performance and combinations of items on these eleven scales, three additional scales can be examined:

- *Pathognomic* : indicates presence of brain dysfunction.

- *Left Hemisphere* : examines right-hand performance.

- *Right Hemisphere* : examines left-hand performance.

To determine the nature and extent of brain damage, neuropsychologists compare LNNB results with estimates of the individual's educational level.

Often, there is a fair amount of overlap between the physician's and the neuropsychologist's assessment procedures. Although such an overlap may be awkward at times, it is ultimately beneficial, as it allows for comparisons by two professionals whose training, experiences, and professional orientations are often vastly different.*

During one week, Dr. V. conducted neuropsychological assessments with:

- A sixty-five-year-old man who is having difficulty remembering important events and people in his life.

- A seventy-five-year-old stroke victim.

---

*For those interested in learning more about neuropsychological assessment, a brief list of current references is provided at the end of this chapter.

- A thirty-five-year-old man who is experiencing difficulty concentrating and sleeping and who has been having nightmares.

Dr. V. performs complete neuropsychological assessments with these clients for two major purposes: (1) to assist in identifying or diagnosing the problem and (2) to attempt to remedy the problem or at least help the clients learn to cope with it. All three of these clients have been referred to Dr. V. for neuropsychological assessments by physicians who have already completed extensive medical testing.

Following his neuropsychological examination of the sixty-five-year-old man with the memory disorder, Dr. V. and the neurologist who conducted the medical examination meet and agree that the client appears to be suffering from symptoms of Alzheimer's disease. Dr. V. meets with the man and his wife, presents his findings to them, and introduces the notion of planning for the future. He gives them the name of a clinical psychologist who specializes in working with Alzheimer's patients and who has recently started a support group for the families of Alzheimer's victims.

With the seventy-five-year-old stroke victim, Dr. V. uses the results of his neuropsychological assesssment to describe the man's current level of functioning. Dr. V. meets with the man's family and suggests that they contact a physical therapist at the hospital who will come to the man's home twice a week to work on strengthening his right hand. Dr. V. also suggests that the family consider a variety of long-term care options for this man. Presently his wife is his primary caretaker, and the couple's three children help when they can. This arrangement is putting a tremendous strain on all four family members. Dr. V. recommends that the family at least visit and consider some of the nursing homes in the area.

In the case of the thirty-five-year-old man experiencing concentration and sleeping difficulties, the results of a thorough neuropsychological examination indicate that the client, a Vietnam War veteran, is suffering from combat-related post-traumatic stress disorder. Dr. V. communicates these findings to the referring physician. Together they suggest to the client an intervention plan involving individual psychotherapy with the psychologist and periodic medical check-ups with the physician. That way, the two professionals can work as a team to ensure the client's optimal progress.

These are examples of the types of cases a clinical psychologist in a VA medical center may see for psychological assessment. Of course, not all clinical psychologists employed by VA medical centers specialize in neuropsychological disorders. Unlike the psychologist in a community mental health center or the psychologist in private practice, the clinical psychologist in a VA center may spend a great deal of time working with patients who cannot function in the outside world and must be hospitalized for an extended period of time. In such cases the psychologist may work as part of a team of health care professionals in meeting the patient's needs. Often the major role of the psychologist in such cases is to conduct periodic psychological assessments to determine the patient's level of functioning and progress in treatment. The psychiatrist may conduct therapy with the patient on a regular basis. As mentioned earlier in this chapter, 36 percent of the psychologists in VA centers surveyed by Lubin et al. (1986a) reported working with more than 500 clients per year, and 17 percent worked with more than 1,000 per year. These psychologists no doubt have time for little beyond a quick initial interview and the administration of a few brief psychological tests.

Ethical Standards for Clinical Psychologists Involved in Psychological Assessment

Clinical psychologists who use psychological tests must adhere to all of the guidelines described in the *Standards for Educational and Psychological Testing* (1985). These standards were prepared by a joint committee with representatives from three organizations—the American Educational Research Association (AERA), the American Psychological Association (APA), and the National Council on Measurement in Education (NCME). Ethical testing practices generally include the following questions:

- What do I want to know?

- Will testing help me to gain this information?

- Is testing the most efficient means of gaining this information?

- Which tests are most appropriate based on the client's age, sex, educational level, race, ethnic background, primary language, and presenting problem?

- What reliability and validity data are available for each of the tests?

- What do I know about the client from the results of the tests that I did not know before?

- Are my test interpretations "hunches" or "facts"?

- How much "clinical judgment" was involved in the evaluation and interpretation of test results?

- With whom and in what form should my findings be shared?

Concluding Remarks

This chapter has illustrated the ways that clinical psychologists use psychological assessment data in three very different settings. Although the same types of tests may be used in all three settings, the purpose for the assessment, the processes involved, and the applications of test results may differ not only from one setting to the next but also within a single setting.

ADDITIONAL READING

For more information about clinical psychology, consult the following sources.

Recent Books

Bernstein, D. A., & Nietzel, M. T. (1980). *Introduction to clinical psychology.* New York: McGraw-Hill.

Karas, E. (Ed.). (1983). *Current issues in clinical psychology.* New York: Plenum Press.

Kendall, P. L., & Norton-Ford, J. D. (1982). *Clinical psychology: Scientific and professional dimensions.* New York: Wiley.

Korchin, S. J. (1976). *Modern clinical psychology: Principles of intervention in the clinic and community.* New York: Basic Books.

Phares, L. J. (1984). *Clinical psychology: Concepts, methods, and profession* (rev. ed.). Homewood, IL: Dorsey Press.

Reisman, J. M. (1976). *The development of clinical psychology.* New York: Appleton-Century-Crofts.

Reisman, J. M. (1976). *A history of clinical psychology.* Enlarged edition. New York: Irvington.

Saccuzzo, D. P., & Kaplan, R. M. (1984). *Clinical psychology.* Boston: Allyn & Bacon.

Sheras, P. L., & Worchel, S. (1979). *Clinical psychology: A social psychological approach.* New York: D. Van Nostrand.

Walker, C. E. (Ed.). (1981). *Clinical practice in psychology.* New York: Pergamon Press.

Weiner, I. B. (Ed.). (1976). *Clinical methods in psychology.* New York: Wiley.

Journals

American Journal of Psychotherapy
Journal of Clinical Psychology
Journal of Consulting and Clinical Psychology
Clinical Psychology Review
The Clinical Psychologist

For more information about community psychology, consult the following sources.

Recent Books

Heller, K., & Monahan, J. (1977). *Psychology and community change.* Homewood, IL: Dorsey Press.

Heller, K., Price, R. H., Reinharz, S., & Wandersman, A. (1984). *Psychology and community change : Challenges of the future.* (2nd ed.). Homewood, IL: Dorsey Press.

Levine, M. (1981). *The history and politics of community mental health.* New York: Oxford University Press.

Mann, P. A. (1978). *Community psychology: Concepts and applications.* New York: Free Press.

Rappaport, J. (1977). *Community psychology: Values, research and action.* New York: Holt, Rinehart & Winston.

Journals

American Journal of Community Psychology
Community Mental Health Journal
Journal of Community Psychology

For more information regarding neuropsychological assessment, consult the following sources.

Recent Books

Benton, A. L., Hamsher, K. D., Verney, N. R., & Spreen, O. (1983). *Contributions to neuropsychological assessment: A clinical manual.* New York: Oxford University Press.

Hecaen, H., & Albert, M. L. (1978). *Human neuropsychology.* New York: John Wiley and Sons.

Heilman, K., & Valenstein, E. (Eds.). (1974). *Clinical neuropsychology.* New York: Oxford University Press.

Hynd, G. W., & Obrzut, J. E. (Eds.). (1981). *Neuropsychological assessment and the school age child: Issues and procedures.* New York: Grune & Stratton.

Kertesz, A. (Ed.). (1983). *Localization in neuropsychology.* New York: Academic Press.

Lezak, M. (1983). *Neuropsychological assessment.* (2nd ed.). New York: Oxford University Press.

Reitan, R. M., & Davison, L. A. (Eds.). (1974). *Clinical neuropsychology: Current status and applications.* Washington, DC: V. H. Winston & Sons.

Wedding, D., Horton, A. M., Webster, J. (Eds.). (1986). *The neuropsychology handbook: Behavioral and clinical perspectives.* New York: Springer Publishing.

CHAPTER 4

Psychological Assessment and the Counseling Psychologist

As mentioned in Chapter 2 counseling psychologists are employed in a wide variety of settings, including university counseling centers, community mental health centers, prisons, hospitals, and military installations. A study by M. Goldschmitt, R. M. Tipton, and R. C. Wiggins (1981) found that the 304 respondents, all members of APA's Division of Counseling Psychology (Division 17), were employed in the following settings and positions:

University (academic department)

University counseling center

Private practice

Community mental health center

Medical and rehabilitation hospital

Administration

Mental hospital

Industry and consultation

In addition, ten respondents reported that they worked in "other" settings not listed.

This vast array of contexts makes it difficult to provide a general assessment-related scenario for the counseling psychologist. To add to the confusion, there are at least nine subspecialties among counseling psychologists: rehabilitation, vocational, educational, employee, marriage/family, personal, pastoral, disabled, and employment. Nonetheless, counseling psychologists often administer psychological tests, using methods that are distinguishable from the procedures employed by psychological personnel in contrasting settings.

Counseling psychologists use tests for two major but not unrelated purposes. First, they use tests to help them better understand each client and to increase the client's level of self-awareness. Second, they may use tests for planning and decision making. To quote L. Goldman (1971): "Counseling psychologists use tests to help individuals know themselves better, and to plan and live their lives as effectively as possible" (p. 1).

In addition, counseling psychologists may use tests to save time in identifying a client's areas of strength and weakness. In other words, psychological tests can provide a standardized observational setting for counseling psychologists to view their clients. These observations can help psychologists see a different "side" of their clients than they might otherwise observe in a nontesting counseling relationship.

Assessment techniques can help the counseling psychologist and the client by:

- Facilitating conversation: Providing a starting point for the counselor and client; serving as an "ice breaker."

- Suggesting a direction for further counseling: Illuminating for the counselor and client the areas in the client's life that need to be improved.

- Opening up new options for the client: Suggesting possible careers or interests that the client had not previously considered; providing the client with alternative strategies for handling problems.

- Evaluating the client's progress: Has the counseling process been effective in "solving" the presenting problem? Increasing self-esteem? Improving decision making?

On a long-term basis, psychological assessment techniques can serve an important research-related function for the counseling psychologist. Test results can greatly facilitate investigations into the effectiveness of specific therapeutic techniques with a variety of clients under different conditions. For example, do females respond better to group counseling than males? How effective are vocational tests in predicting on-the-job success? Do preventive programs such as those dealing with substance abuse have an impact on adolescent decision making?

The section titled "Test Use in Counseling" in the *Standards for Educational and Psychological Testing* (1985) mentions an interesting notion: "Uses of tests in counseling differ from most other test uses in that the test taker is viewed as the primary user of test results" (p. 55). In other words, the primary reason for testing in schools, businesses, and industries may be to determine an individual's qualifications for anything from a special education placement to a particular job. In a counseling setting, the main reason for testing is for test takers to learn more about themselves. The counseling psychologist is a facilitator in the testing process rather than a "gatekeeper" to educational or employment opportunities.

Institutional and administrative constraints exist for counseling psychologists in all settings, with the possible exception of private practice. For example, a counseling psychologist might be expected to work with a minimum number of individual clients per year, thus limiting the amount of time she may spend with any one client. In addition, a counseling psychologist might have a wide array of duties listed in priority order on a job description. The list may place individual psychological testing well below vocational planning, group testing, group and individual counseling, or staff development. Also, it may include guidelines regarding the uses of particular types of assessment techniques (for example, vocational tests may be emphasized over individualized tests of intelligence). Finally, even the most progressive and flexible agency may lack the financial resources for ordering tests not already available.

What Psychological Tests Do Counseling Psychologists Use?

One recent study (Fee, Elkins, & Boyd, 1982) asked 500 members of APA Division 17 (Counseling Psychology) to list those tests they felt students in counseling psychology training programs should learn to administer. Respondents listed three tests more often than any others: the Minnesota Multiphasic Personality Inventory, the Wechsler Adult Intelligence Scale, and the Strong-Campbell Interest Inventory. The authors (Fee et al.) point out that the inclusion of one personality test, one intelligence test, and one vocational-interest inventory "emphasizes the necessity for counseling psychology students to become well versed with a diversity of testing instruments" (p. 117). Other tests mentioned (but much less frequently) were the Wechsler Intelligence Scale for Children—Revised, the Thematic Apperception Test, the Bender-Gestalt test, the Rorschach, and the Stanford-Binet. The psychologists in the survey administered objective tests to slightly more than one third of their clients and projective tests to slightly more than one tenth. The three most frequent reasons for testing in this study were: to obtain vocational and career-related information, to aid in the diagnosis of psychopathology, and to assess the client's intellectual functioning. Fee et al. asked respondents what alternatives to traditional psychological testing they employed. Respondents offering specific alternatives most often mentioned the use of clinical interviewing and behavioral observation techniques. Other respondents mentioned the importance of integrating all available information and records about the client and making use of "information derived from the counseling relationship" (p. 117) as part of a thorough assessment process.

A second examination of the use of psychological tests in counseling (Zytowski & Warman, 1982) yielded different findings than the Fee et al. (1982) study. Zytowski and Warman assessed the reported use of 95 test instruments within

198 counseling agencies. This total consisted of 99 college and university coun-seling services, 84 private counseling agencies, and 15 counseling services at community and junior colleges. Overall, the test used more often than any other by the majority of the agencies was the Strong-Campbell Interest Inven-tory (SCII). Other frequently used tests included the Kuder Occupational Interest Survey (ranked 2), the Edwards Personal Preference Schedule (3), the Nelson-Denny Reading Test (4), the Sixteen Personality Factors (5), the Self-Directed Search (6), the Wechsler Adult Intelligence Scale (7), the American College Test-ing Assessment (8), the Survey of Study Habits and Attitudes (9), and the Minne-sota Multiphasic Personality Inventory (10).

The Zytowski and Warman (1982) study noted marked differences in test usage based on setting. Community and junior college counseling centers used psychological tests least often, while public and private agencies used them most frequently. Zytowski and Warman did not address the reason for this difference.

The difference in findings between the Fee et al. study and the Zytowski and Warman study may be partially attributable to their respective methodolo-gies. Fee asked counseling psychologists what assessment techniques they would recommend students in counseling training programs learn to administer. Zytow-ski and Warman, on the other hand, examined actual testing practices within counseling agencies. Their study was not limited to counseling psychologists but included a broader range of individuals performing counseling-related services.

The Role of the Client in the Testing Process

Counseling psychology views the client as a rational, healthy person who is having difficulty with a particular problem. It makes sense, therefore, that the counseling psychologist should engage the client as much as possible in the treatment process itself. She should have a say in the nature and outcome of treatment including which, if any, types of tests to take. Because the client is usually unfamiliar with psychological assessment techniques, the psychologist will frequently need to provide information about the advantages and disadvan-tages of various tests.

In his book *Using Tests in Counseling*, L. Goldman (1971) cautions coun-selors not to think of psychological tests as objective tools. He emphasizes that for the person taking the test, awaiting the results, and particularly receiving the results, testing is anything but an objective experience. Goldman advises that during all phases of psychological testing "attention should be paid to the same basic principles which apply to all counseling activities" (p. 40). Counseling psychologists should maintain and communicate their "unconditional positive regard" (that is, their acceptance and understanding) for the client during assessment procedures just as they would during any other counseling-related activity.

To illustrate this principle, Goldman encourages counselors, whenever possible, to select tests *with* the client rather than *for* the client. In this way clients will learn more about themselves, and counselors can observe their clients' strengths and weaknesses and discuss their decision-making processes. In addition, clients' participation in test selection may increase their independence and reduce their indecisiveness. Of course, decisions about specific tests may be best left to the professional familiar with psychometric properties (norms, reliability, and validity of the available instruments). Most clients, however, can participate to some extent in selecting the types of tests and in choosing the most beneficial reporting of results.

Consider how two types of counseling psychologists employ assessment techniques in their work settings. In the first example, Dr. A. works in a university counseling center. In the second example, Dr. B. works as a rehabilitation counselor.

● ● ● ● ● ●

EXAMPLE 4.1

THE COUNSELING PSYCHOLOGIST IN A UNIVERSITY COUNSELING CENTER

Most readers of this book should not find it difficult to identify with college students seeking counseling. For the so-called traditional college student, eighteen to twenty-two years of age, there are important decisions to be made—decisions that may shape much of adult life. What should I major in? What about a minor? Should I apply to a graduate or professional school? If so, what are my chances of being admitted? Why don't I have more friends? Why don't I have more dates? Should I get married now or wait until I'm through with school? For the "nontraditional" college student, additional concerns related to aging, parenting, and going to school part-time may add stress to the college experience.

These questions and problems are difficult enough to answer, and we have not yet even mentioned family problems, health problems, eating disorders, substance abuse, roommate conflicts, and many other events with crisis potential. It is hardly surprising that psychological service centers on college campuses rarely lack clients.

Counseling psychologists are frequently employed by university or college counseling centers. Depending on the types and numbers of other services available on and off campus and the extent of available funding, these centers may attempt to facilitate the educational, personal, social, and vocational development of the students. Psychological assessment can play an important role in this process. Consider some of the clients a psychologist in a university counseling center might see in a typical day.

9:00

Mike was waiting by the doors of the counseling center fifteen minutes before it opened. He is a sophomore majoring in pre-engineering. Yesterday he got an F on a test in his differential equations class, and he is not doing very well in physics, either. Mike has a feeling that engineering may not have been a good decision, but he doesn't know what else to choose. At this point in his life, graduate school sounds dreadful, but so does getting a job. Even if he were to choose a field requiring postcollege training, Mike would need a great deal of financial help in order to pursue this advanced education. He has come to the counseling center for help in deciding what to do and how to proceed.

Dr. A., the counseling psychologist, would probably try to summarize Mike's situation to clarify the major themes for their mutual benefit. She might say something like, "From what you've told me, it sounds as though you are facing some major decisions, and might like to talk them over with me to help you decide. Also, you might like some insight into your strengths and weaknesses for potential careers, and about graduate study if that seems necessary in meeting your career goals. If it is necessary, you will need to know about the types of financial assistance available and the qualifications needed for such assistance. Does that sound about right? Did I omit anything?"

If Mike agrees with her summary, Dr. A. might suggest testing to help clarify Mike's academic and personal strengths and weaknesses and to provide some career guidance for Mike. In order to address Mike's questions Dr. A. might arrange for him to take the following tests. (Note that these tests take a long time and would not be given during this first appointment.)

- The Wechsler Adult Intelligence Scale-Revised (WAIS-R). Dr. A. might personally administer the WAIS-R to Mike. This would allow her not only to learn more about Mike's intellectual abilities but also to observe Mike's behavior under the standardized conditions of testing.

- The Strong-Campbell Interest Inventory (SCII). The SCII was developed to facilitate educational and vocational planning in adolescents and adults. Based on a computer analysis of Mike's responses to the 325 multiple-choice items, Dr. A. and Mike can try to match Mike's strengths, weaknesses, likes, and dislikes with general occupational categories and even with some specific career options.

Following the administration and scoring of Mike's WAIS-R and SCII protocols (test booklets) Dr. A. wrote the following summary:

Name: **Mike** _____   <u>Age</u>: **20 years, 2 months**
<u>Major</u>: **Pre-engineering**   <u>Year</u> <u>in</u> <u>School</u>: **Sophomore**

<u>Referral Question(s)</u>:

1. What career goals would be most appropriate?
2. How should he go about achieving these goals?

<u>Results of Testing</u>:

On the Wechsler Adult Intelligence Scale—Revised, Mike scored within the superior range (120-130) overall. He scored somewhat higher on performance tasks such as block designs than on verbal tasks, although the difference was not statistically significant. He was quite consistent on all subtests. His lowest scaled score (10) was on vocabulary. All other scaled scores on verbal subtests were either 11 or 12. On the performance tests, he had scaled scores of 12 on all subtests but block design and object assembly. On these subtests he scored 14.

Mike's behavior during testing showed consistent and diligent effort. He was flexible in his approach to the performance tasks and kept working until he achieved what he considered the correct solution, always finishing within the time limits set by the test developer. On the verbal tasks, Mike did not answer impulsively. He carefully considered questions before responding. He paid attention and rarely had to ask the examiner to repeat a question. Overall, Mike's performance on the WAIS-R indicates a thoughtful response style to questions and a high level of intellectual ability.

Following the WAIS-R administration, Mike completed the Strong-Campbell Interest Inventory (SCII). The computer analysis of his performance on the SCII indicates that Mike had scores of very high on the I-(Investigative) theme and on the S-(Social) theme. He scored at the moderately high level on the R-(Realistic) and C-(Conventional) theme. Finally, he scored within the average range on the A-(Artistic) and E-(Enterprising) themes.

After studying the list of careers that match his theme scores most closely, Mike decides to investigate the educational requirements and job descriptions for the following occupations: mathematics teacher, engineer, computer programmer, medical technologist, and nurse. In his fourth and final appointment with Dr. A., Mike discusses his plans to learn more about these occupations. Dr. A. wishes him well, encourages him to keep her informed of his progress, and lets him know that if he needs counseling services in the future, he should feel free to stop in.

Carol enters the psychologist's office without making eye contact with Dr. A. Her eyes are red, and she appears to have been crying. Dr. A. waits for a minute or two, but Carol does not say anything, so Dr. A breaks the ice.

DR. A.: I can see something is upsetting you. How may I help you?

CAROL (between sobs): Everything is going wrong. I'm a freshman—the first person in my family to go to college. My parents keep telling me how lucky I am to be here and how they know I'll do fine. I wish I had as much faith in myself as they have in me.

My classes are hard. My roommate has a boyfriend who comes to visit every weekend and stays in our room. I can't sleep, I can't study, I haven't made any friends. My parents don't make it any easier—when I try to tell them how miserable I am they just tell me that things will get better, it just takes time. I don't know what to do.

Dr. A. would try to summarize Carol's words and feelings.

DR. A.: It sounds as though nothing is going well in your life at the moment. You feel like you have no direction and nowhere to turn—your parents don't understand; your friends from home are far away; there's no one here that you feel close to.

I think you made a good decision to come here. We can talk things over and work out some strategies to improve or at least help you cope with some of the difficulties you are facing. Where would you like to start? What do you see as the biggest problem right now?

CAROL: My roommate and her boyfriend. She's okay by herself during the week, but when they're together, I'm uncomfortable. They've asked me to go places with them, but I don't want to just tag along. On the weekends he stays in our room, so I have to find somewhere else to sleep and study. I tried to talk to her about this, but she says she doesn't know what else to do. They're in love and want to spend all their weekends together, and since she doesn't have a car, he comes to see her. They can't afford a motel room.

Dr. A. would probably work on a couple of areas with Carol—perhaps assertiveness training and problem-solving skills. She might even consider having her join an assertiveness group to help her make some friends and develop the support system she seems to be looking for.

With Carol's presenting problems, it is likely that no formal testing is needed. It should be emphasized that an important step in the assessment process is knowing when testing is unnecessary or inappropriate as well as knowing what tests to give when they are needed. Whether or not to test is a complicated matter; a number of questions should be considered before deciding:

- What do I want to know?

- How can I obtain the information most efficiently and effectively?

- Is there a test that addresses this question?

- If so, is it available to me and appropriate for this client, and am I qualified to administer it?

- Will I gain anything from testing that I would not acquire through a clinical interview?

11:00

Roger enters Dr. A.'s office carrying a folder that he promptly hands to Dr. A. Before glancing through the file, Dr. A asks Roger how she can help him.

ROGER: I'm a senior in high school. I have a learning disability that makes it hard for me to read. My high school counselor told me to talk to a college counselor to see what kinds of services are available for a college student with learning disabilities. Also, do you have special admission requirements for L.D. students? She thought that maybe you could give me an IQ test or something like it instead of my having to take the ACT in a group. Group tests are always terrible for me. The individual and group tests I've had during elementary school and high shool are all described in that folder. I do okay on anything that doesn't involve much reading.

DR. A: Let me make sure I've got this right. You would like to go to college, possibly here, after you graduate from high school. You want to know, first, if you are admissible and second, if you do get admitted, what services are available to help you succeed. Is that it?

ROGER: Well, those are the most important questions at the moment. If you have time, though, I could also use some help in choosing a career. I'm not sure what choices are available for a person with a reading problem.

DR. A. (leafing through Roger's folder): It looks as though you've taken a lot of tests. I will need to spend some time going over these test results to see if we need any additional information to determine your eligibility, placement needs, and vocational options. We do have other students enrolled here with learning disabilities, and they have a kind of support group. Would you like to meet with them and hear about the campus from their perspective?

ROGER: That sounds great. I could use some support.

DR. A.: Let's proceed in two ways. First, I'll look through your folder and outline what additional tests, if any, might be helpful. Second, the support

Psychological Assessment and the Counseling Psychologist **61** group meets today at four. I'll call the leader and ask him if you can attend. I'm sure it will be fine, but I'd like to double check anyway. How about if we meet at about three-thirty, plan the testing, and then I'll introduce you to the other group members?

ROGER: I'll be here at three-thirty. See you then.

After looking through Roger's folder, Dr. A. decides that the following information would be most helpful:

1. An up-to-date measure of ability, probably an individually administered IQ test like the WAIS-R (an advantage of such individually administered tests is that they require little, if any, reading).

2. An up-to-date diagnostic test of reading, spelling, math, and other school-related skills.

3. A vocational interest scale (perhaps the SCII).

So, there we have one morning of Dr. A.'s schedule. Of the three students, testing seemed necessary for two and unwarranted for the third. After administering and scoring the tests, Dr. A. would meet quickly with Mike and with Roger to share the results and to help them develop their academic and vocational future plans.

Mike's best course of action seemed to be to investigate those areas in which he scored high in terms of undergraduate requirements, postgraduate education, and so forth. Dr. A. might become a liaison or resource person for Mike, suggesting people on or off campus to contact or places to visit.

For Roger, testing might indicate his qualifications for admission to the university. Dr. A. might act as a student advocate with Roger's professors, arranging for someone to take notes for him, urging that lectures and textbooks be audiotaped, and that Roger be given examinations orally.

Dr. A.'s morning caseload illustrates several important roles and principles critical to counseling psychology. First, she displayed acceptance and respect for all three clients. She was in no way judgmental or insincere. Second, she took a problem-solving approach to helping all three clients. Instead of delving into covert motives, Dr. A.'s approach was more flexible: "If this is the situation you are facing, here are some alternatives for us to pursue." Dr. A. focused on working through the present problem while building some mechanisms to help in the future. For Mike, selecting a vocational goal for which he is better suited may be all that is needed. For Carol and Roger, however, part of Dr. A.'s strategy was to get them involved in support groups to help them cope with future circumstances or situations. It is likely that Dr. A. leads one or both groups as part of her job. Third, Dr. A. did not use testing as a panacea. She suggested testing in two of the three cases as merely one step in a problem-solving process. She also knew that testing was probably not warranted in Carol's case. The test results for Mike and Roger may enable both young men to increase their self-awareness and to derive maximum benefit from their college years.

Some college and university counseling centers employ a more specialized approach than the one just described. Such centers may have one person designated as the test administrator. Any psychological assessments that others on the staff request are referred to that person. The test administrator then gives the results to the referring psychologist to incorporate into the total counseling process. Although this approach allows one person to become a genuine expert in psychological testing, having someone else test Dr. A.'s clients would have prevented Dr. A. from observing Mike and Roger during the testing process itself. •

• • • • • •

EXAMPLE 4.2

THE COUNSELING PSYCHOLOGIST SPECIALIZING IN REHABILITATION OR GERONTOLOGY

As has been mentioned several times, counseling psychologists work in many different settings. Dr. A.'s caseload at a university counseling center would undoubtedly be vastly different from that of a rehabilitation or a gerontological counselor.

According to A. Anastasi (1979) and others, the rehabilitation counselor's role centers around meeting the needs of disabled individuals. The counselor might coordinate schedules and goals for physical, occupational, and speech therapy as well as for any medical services an individual requires. It is not unusual for him to provide some financial counseling to clients and their families as well.

In addition, the rehabilitation counselor works with the clients and others in the client's environment (family, friends, and other caretakers), in developing realistic attitudes toward the disabling condition. It is common for people experiencing permanently or even temporarily disabling conditions to become frustrated and depressed. Clients may show painfully slow progress at best, and many experience setbacks. Some clients suffer from degenerative conditions— illnesses that become increasingly serious or life-threatening.

Under what circumstances would a rehabilitation counseling psychologist use psychological tests? The primary application of tests might center around occupational or vocational assessment. At what level is the individual currently functioning? What is the individual capable of doing? How compatible is a particular vocational goal with the individual's prognosis? What effects would a specific vocational choice have on the client's self-esteem?

Another useful category of psychological tests are the so-called scales of adaptive behavior. Such scales measure a person's abilities to cope with daily living. Behaviors that might be included are self-help skills (washing, dressing, feeding); communication skills (talking, listening, understanding); and occupational skills (purchasing items, being responsible). Administering this scale provides a concrete measure of an individual's ability to cope without assistance. Usually, adaptive scales are administered to a third party who is familiar with the client—a parent, spouse, or other caretaker.

Many specific tests have been developed or adapted for particular disabling conditions. Tests are designed for the deaf and hearing impaired, for the blind and visually impaired, and for those with orthopedic disabilities. Certainly, rehabilitation psychologists should be familiar with these assessment instruments as well.

Some counseling psychologists might choose to specialize in **gerontology**, the study of aging and the special problems of the elderly. Unlike other specialties within counseling psychology, the psychologist working as a gerontology counselor typically does not spend much time engaged in psychological testing. Gerontological counselors tend to focus on the individual's adjustment to aging. Just as families and friends of disabled persons may occasionally need professional counseling and adjustment, those close to the elderly may also need such services. It is not easy for a once hearty and independent person to become increasingly frail and dependent. It may be just as difficult for that person's children to become responsible for the once seemingly omnipotent parent. All of these people may need counseling and support. Gerontological counseling is in great need of research, and psychological assessment may be most useful in this area. What should a person expect with increasing age? What common problems do the elderly face? What factors relate to positive adjustment and resilience? These questions and many others must be answered as people live longer and as the proportion of the elderly in our population continues to grow.

One area of psychological testing with applications to the elderly is neuropsychological testing. Briefly, neuropsychological testing examines brain-behavior relationships (see Chapter 3 for a lengthier description). The elderly may experience many neurological disorders with vast psychological ramifications, (for example, strokes, Alzheimer's disease, or Parkinson's disease). What may be especially distressing about such disorders is that their damage may not be limited to physiological changes. In addition to partial paralysis, incontinence, and so forth, the person may undergo tremendous emotional and intellectual changes as a direct result of the disorder. A once-docile individual may become difficult and stubborn; a once-rational person may begin to hallucinate; and a once-brilliant person may have difficulty recalling the letters of the alphabet. Physical changes are often much easier to cope with than these psychological changes.

Neuropsychological testing can help treat these disorders in at least three ways. First, it can pinpoint the afflicted areas to some extent. Second, it can be useful in demonstrating to the individual's family that the personality changes are indeed part of the disorder. Finally, as with many other aspects of psychological testing, neuropsychological testing is needed for research purposes—to increase our understanding of brain-behavior relationships. •

Ethical Considerations for the Counseling Psychologist Using Psychological Assessment

Within the field of counseling psychology, a client usually seeks the psychologist's help with a particular problem or question. What career should I pursue? How can I become more assertive in my relationships? What should my major be in college? What am I capable of achieving? Psychological testing should relate directly to these questions. As with all testing, the counseling psychologist has an ethical responsibility to use tests and other assessment tools that are relevant and recent. That is, they must be appropriate for the individual client, they must relate to his or her concerns, and they must be current given the "state of the art" in psychology. Psychologists may share results only with the client or those designated by the client. They must be knowledgeable about the interpretation of test results and must clearly explain them to clients.

Concluding Remarks

Counseling psychology is an area that includes a large and diverse group of subspecialties. Its major concern is problem exploration and solving. Psychological assessment can often facilitate the problem exploration phase while simultaneously suggesting tentative answers or solutions. Such assessment procedures can enhance—but not replace—the psychologist-client relationship.

ADDITIONAL READING

For more information about counseling psychology, consult the following sources.

Recent Books

Blocher, D. H., & Biggs, D. A. (1983). *Counseling psychology in community settings.* New York: Springer.

Boy, A. V., & Pine, G. J. (1982). *Client-centered counseling: A renewal.* Boston: Allyn & Bacon.

Brammer, L. M., & Shostrum, E. L. (1982). *Therapeutic psychology: Fundamentals of counseling and psychotherapy* (4th ed.). Englewood Cliffs, NJ: Prentice-Hall.

Brown, S. D., & Lent, R. W. (1984). *Handbook of counseling psychology.* New York: John Wiley and Sons.

Corey, G. (1986). *Theory and practice of counseling and psychotherapy* (3rd ed.). Monterey, CA: Brooks/Cole.

Hansen, J. C., Stevic, R. R., & Warner, R. W., Jr. (1982). *Counseling: Theory and process* (3rd ed.). Boston: Allyn & Bacon.

Ivey, A. E., & Simek-Downing, L. (1980). *Counseling and psychotherapy: Skills, theories, and practice.* Englewood Cliffs, NJ: Prentice-Hall.

Kottler, J. A., & Brown, R. W. (1985). *Introduction to therapeutic counseling.* Monterey, CA: Brooks/Cole.

Osipow, S. H., Walsh, W. B., & Tosi, D. J. (1984). *A survey of counseling methods.* Homewood, IL: Dorsey Press.

Patterson, C. H. (1980). *Theories of counseling and psychotherapy* (3rd ed.). New York: Harper & Row.

Patterson, L. E., & Eisenberg, S. (1983). *The counseling process.* Boston: Houghton Mifflin.

Pietrofesa, J., Hoffman, A., & Splete, H. (1984). *Counseling: An introduction.* Boston: Houghton Mifflin.

Shertzer, B., & Stone, S. (1980). *Fundamentals of counseling.* Boston: Houghton Mifflin.

Stone, G. L. (1986). *Counseling psychology: Perspectives and issues.* Monterey, CA: Brooks/Cole.

VanHoose, W. H., & Kottler, J. A. (1985). *Ethical and legal issues in counseling and psychotherapy* (2nd ed.). San Francisco: Jossey-Bass.

Whiteley, J. M. (1980). *History of counseling psychology.* Washington, DC: AACD Press.

Whiteley, J. M., & Fretz, B. R. (1980). *The present and future of counseling psychology.* Washington, DC: AACD Press.

Journals

Counseling Psychologist
Journal of Counseling Psychology
Personnel and Guidance Journal

Psychological Assessment and the Industrial/ Organizational Psychologist

When we think of large businesses and industries, it is easy to lose sight of the fact that these organizations are really groups of individuals working together. The effectiveness of each of these individuals has an impact on the effectiveness of other individuals and ultimately on the functioning of the organization as a whole. Focusing on the importance of each individual in the overall functioning of an organization, it is not difficult to imagine how a psychologist's skills and training might be useful to that organization. This chapter will emphasize the ways in which industrial/organizational (I/O) psychologists employ tests and other assessment procedures in businesses and industries in an effort to improve their functioning. It will examine the I/O psychologist's role in personnel selection and will also focus on legal and ethical issues surrounding the use of tests. It should be noted that most tests used by I/O psychologists are group tests rather than individually administered diagnostic tests.

Selection of New Personnel

At one time or another nearly every business needs one or more employees. Larger organizations may enlist I/O psychologists to help them in their personnel searches. Sometimes these psychologists are already employed by the organization. At other times an I/O psychologist may be brought in as a consultant especially for the purpose of personnel selection. Although the hiring of new personnel may appear to be a simple and straightforward matter, in reality it is anything but simple. Several steps are generally involved in finding the right person for a particular job. The I/O psychologist may or may not be involved in all of them. All steps are included below, however, to show where the I/O psychologist's skills fit into the total personnel selection process.

Step 1: Determination of Needs

In some industries when an employee leaves or is moved to another job or location, an immediate replacement is needed to perform a specific function. For example, someone is needed to perform a task on an assembly line or to manage the switchboard. These obvious gaps must be filled quickly to meet daily demands and maintain the organization's effectiveness. Describing needs in such cases is a matter of putting into words the work that must be done.

In other cases, however, the determination of needs is much more complicated. Let us take the department of psychology at a large university as an example. One professor retires and a second moves to a position at another university. The retiring professor taught courses in psychology of personality and senior-level seminars in Jung and Adler. The other professor taught courses in organizational behavior, applied psychology, and psychological testing. Should the department replace these individuals with others in the same areas of training and expertise or should some effort be made to determine whether individuals in these same areas would best meet departmental needs? Have student needs and interests changed over time? Has the field of psychology changed so that new courses should be added and existing courses deleted? What sort of new faculty member would complement the teaching and research interests of current faculty? How would a change in curriculum affect existing faculty and courses?

Universities are not the only organizations with such complex decisions to make. Businesses change—they may require a person with sophisticated knowledge of computer technology rather than a person with more traditional secretarial or bookkeeping skills. On the other hand, they may want to concentrate on new product lines requiring personnel with different skills to design, develop, and implement the new ideas. They may hire a new president with ideas and expectations for "middle-management" individuals different from those of previous administrators.

These changes require skillful analyses. Although I/O psychologists may not be involved in this step of the hiring process, they may be quite instrumental in assessing the needs of an organization and determining the types and level of skills required for potential employees. The I/O psychologist's input at this stage can greatly influence the future of the organization.

Step 2: Obtaining Permission to Hire

Once an organization's personnel needs have been determ'
may be to convince those in power that such needs do, ir
resources should be allocated to meet them. Although it n
gician would be more useful than a psychologist in accomplisn.. ᴄ
I/O psychologist, skilled in interpersonal communication and organizatioᴜ..
velopment and armed with good solid data regarding the organization's needs,
could be invaluable in obtaining permission to hire new employees. I/O psychologists are frequently not involved in this step; obtaining permission to hire
personnel is often left to a personnel manager or other employee within an
organization.

Step 3: Job Analysis and Description

The third step in the selection process is highly dependent on assessment procedures. Job analysis and description can be conveniently divided into two
smaller steps:

a. Describing the tasks performed on the job.

b. Determining the skills or characteristics that make one person successful
and another unsuccessful at a particular job.

In her book *Fields of Applied Psychology* (1979), A. Anastasi suggests several useful procedures for accomplishing these two steps. Some of the procedures can be thought of as **indirect** assessment techniques. For the I/O psychologist, indirect techniques may involve looking at the company's records,
checking the most recent edition of the *Dictionary of Occupational Titles*, talking to people inside the organization (but not those who actually perform the
job being considered), and talking to people at similar organizations.

Direct assessment techniques, on the other hand, may include observing
or interviewing individuals already performing the job in question. Employees
performing a particular job may be asked to keep daily logs of their duties and
functions or to keep more informal records of their work. Workers may be
asked to complete structured surveys that ask questions about job-related variables, such as allocation of time on various tasks.

Organizations have developed more formal systems of job analysis. One
system, the **Task Assessment Scales**, examines the specific motor activities or
abilities needed to perform a particular job. Examples of motor activities include reaction time, finger dexterity, and arm-hand steadiness. Any job can be
classified using these scales to determine the motor abilities needed for success.

Of course, there is more to most jobs than just motor abilities. A second
and much more comprehensive classification system is the **Position Analysis
Questionnaire** (PAQ). The 182 job elements on the PAQ checklist have been

ced (through a statistical procedure known as factor analysis) to six major categories of activities (Marquardt & McCormick, 1974):

1. *Information input activities:* The worker acquires information from the environment.

2. *Mental processes activities:* The worker uses information in decision making.

3. *Output activities:* The worker performs some activity that leads to a change, such as tuning a machine.

4. *Interpersonal activities:* The skills involved in working with or supervising other people.

5. *Job concept:* The impact of the job on the worker, for example, stresses.

6. *Miscellaneous:* The practical or logistical aspects of the job (schedule).

Assessment techniques such as the Task Assessment Scales and the Position Analysis Questionnaire may become increasingly important in the future. As the trend away from general aptitude testing continues, there will be a need for tests that measure the precise tasks for a particular job and the abilities of job candidates to perform those tasks. Such tests will greatly reduce the subjectivity of personnel selection practices.

Step 4: Recruitment of Candidates (Affirmative Action)

The recruitment of candidates for a particular job may involve a variety of procedures. Advertising a job opening in the local "Help Wanted" ads is probably the most common form of recruitment. But it is not unusual to hear about a job opening through word of mouth, from an employment agency, in a placement office at a college or university, or even over the radio or television. Recruitment procedures should, of course, be aimed at the type of person a business hopes to attract. For example, large businesses will often send recruiters to college campuses to interview college seniors for entry-level white-collar jobs. Professional positions are often advertised in journals or other publications that reach a large number of qualified applicants.

In the past several years there has been an increasing sensitivity to the discriminatory recruitment, hiring, and promotion practices of many institutions. Are female and minority job candidates genuinely given equal employment opportunities? At the recruitment stage it is important to make sure that qualified minority candidates find out about job opportunities. A large institution or organization, especially one receiving monies from federal or state governments, often hires an individual to act as the official affirmative action monitor. This person's job is to keep the institution in compliance with federal and state statutes regarding employment practices. At the recruitment stage, this involves making sure that qualified female and minority candidates are given every opportunity to find out about and to apply for all available positions. As with steps 1 and 2, I/O psychologists are rarely involved in the recruitment stage and affirmative-action procedures of the personnel selection process.

Step 5: Selection of Applicants

The goal in personnel selection is to choose the "right" person for a particular job. The I/O psychologist is usually most involved in this step and uses a number of assessment procedures to facilitate this selection process. What information might be useful? The sources of data might include (but are not by any means limited to): application forms, interviews, recommendations, psychological tests, and assessment centers.

Application Forms A careful examination of most job applications or resumes can provide clues about the applicant's attention to detail, spelling and grammar skills, and ability to follow instructions. Is the information correct? Are there unaccounted for gaps in the individual's education and employment history? Does the person meet the minimum qualifications for the job? Occasionally employers may infer too much from the application form and from their own often unsubstantiated notions of the job's requirements. College graduates may be dismisssed as overqualified, while high school dropouts are rejected as underqualified for a job in which level of education is not important (Siegel & Lane, 1982).

Anyone involved in personnel-related matters should know not to ask on an application or in an interview personal questions that have nothing to do with an applicant's job qualifications. Questions pertaining to marital status, number and ages of children, religion, race, sex, and age do not belong on application blanks unless it can be clearly demonstrated that such criteria predict a candidate's job performance. It is easy to see how responses to such questions could eliminate a qualified applicant from serious consideration.

Some personal characteristics, however, can be relied upon to predict job performance. For example, married workers may remain at a job longer than single workers, or college graduates may be more successful in management positions than high school graduates. Organizations may consequently focus their recruitment efforts on married, college graduates. Although there are some serious problems with this procedure—mainly that the exceptions to the rule may not be given equal consideration—the advantages are considerable in terms of money and time invested in the orientation of new employees.

In an effort to maximize their chances of hiring an individual who will be successful on the job and will remain with the organization, many employers use weighted biographical inventories, or **Biodata Forms**, such as the Biographical Information Blank (BIB). These forms grade and assign weights to the applicant's responses based on statistical information. For example, if college graduates have been more successful than high school graduates in management-level positions, the response "college graduate" would yield a higher weighted score than "high school graduate." Such weightings must be frequently "revalidated" to insure that they continue to predict success.

Interviews Why would an applicant be interviewed before being considered for a job? The truthful answer probably is that most of us believe we are pretty good judges of other people's character. Certainly an interview provides additional clues about a job candidate that application forms may not reveal:

- Was the person on time?

- Was the person dressed neatly and appropriately for a job interview?

- Did the person initiate conversation? Have to be "drawn out"? Attempt to control or dominate the conversation?

- How did this person behave compared to others in the same situation? More or less confident?

- What questions did the person ask?

- Did the person seem interested in the job?

Although statistical evidence does not support their predictive validity (Ulrich & Trumbo, 1965), interviews continue to be a popular part of the personnel selection process. As mentioned in Chapter 1, interviews may be highly structured (questions are standardized for all applicants) or highly unstructured (no standardized questions).

Sometimes businesses purposefully introduce additional stress into the already inherently stressful interview situation. I have heard reports of such "stress interviews" from individuals applying to clinical psychology graduate programs and for law enforcement positions. Stress interviews measure how applicants react under uncomfortable and anxiety-producing circumstances.

How "fair" are personnel interviews? This question is the subject of much debate and investigation. According to Goldstein and Krasner (1987), many variables make interview data questionable at best as a source of predictive validity. These include initial bias on the part of the interviewer; the interviewer's gender, age, and physical attractiveness; the previous interviewees (Was the person who was interviewed immediately before the current candidate a strong or weak job contender?); and the interviewee's gender, age, response style, training and experience with interviews, and major field of study.

Recommendations The candidate's letters of reference can yield even more information:

- Who are the letters from? Is there one from the most recent employer?

- Are they positive, negative, or neutral?

- Are there any "trends" in the letters? For example, do they all mention a tendency to be stubborn or a difficulty in accepting responsibility?

The experienced reader can learn a great deal from letters of reference. For example, most job applicants seem to be able to pick people who will write them either neutral or glowing letters of recommendation. A neutral letter says something like "Seth was a student in my Introduction to Psychology class during fall semester, 1986. Although I do not know him well, he performed consistently at the B+ level in the class. I recommend him to you for your consideration." A glowing letter says, "Seth is one of the brightest, most ambitious, and most responsible students our department has ever had. He has earned my highest recommendation."

Occasionally, someone will write a letter saying something like the following: "Seth has become much less belligerent over the years. Although he is still quite defensive when test papers are returned, he has learned to wait until after class to air his views to the professor. It is too bad that Seth is so hot-tempered. He is such a bright and hardworking young man that he could have a great future in almost any field were it not for his inability to take any form of criticism. Under the present circumstances, I cannot recommend him to you except to offer strong words of caution."

Because most letters of reference tend to be positive or at least neutral, a negative letter is a sign of trouble. Employers may use such a letter to make an immediate decision not to offer Seth a job. On the other hand, because most applicants are able to obtain positive letters of recommendation, their value is extremely limited. Five job candidates with five positive letters will not speed up the selection process.

Psychological Tests In addition to using data from applications, interviews, and letters of recommendation in job-related decisions, many businesses and industries use some sort of psychological test data. Some organizations routinely require job applicants to complete a test battery. For certain jobs, there may be cutoff scores that immediately eliminate some candidates from the job competition. Other organizations may weigh test results with the rest of the assessment data to arrive at a more comprehensive prediction of on-the-job success.

Psychological tests have certain advantages over other personnel selection procedures. They have been developed with an emphasis on the critical notions of validity and reliability. You will recall that validity examines whether a test measures what it is supposed to measure, and reliability examines the consistency of a test. Although no test is perfectly reliable or valid for all purposes, at least the validity and reliability coefficients and related data are available to test consumers. Compare psychological tests to most of the other procedures in the hiring process (for example, letters of recommendation or personal interviews), and the tests are far superior for objectivity and standardization. Of course, their validity and reliability depend on the person taking the test as well as the nature of the job to be filled.

What kinds of psychological tests are administered as part of an employee selection process? For practical, ethical, and legal reasons, the answer must depend on the particular job.

From a practical standpoint, consider the costs versus the benefits of psychological tests. Is the expense (in time and money) of administering and scoring one or more tests worth the information acquired? Do the tests help select the right candidate for the job? Do we know more about a person after the test than we knew before? Is the person who scores highest on a test always the best person in the actual job situation? Do we have tests to address all areas of competence?

Most people would agree that giving a typing test to an applicant for a typing job is money and time well spent. If a job applicant types six words a minute with eight errors, an employer would not want to waste time even considering that person for the job. Nor would we want to hire an individual with poor computational skills for a bookkeeping job. Tests of specific abilities and aptitudes for particular jobs are usually cost-efficient and rarely questioned for ethical or legal reasons. A comprehensive job analysis can be invaluable in determining what skills should be assessed.

On the other hand, is an MMPI or a Rorschach test for a secretarial candidate an appropriate use of psychological testing? Does an applicant for a clerical job at the post office need to take a group-administered intelligence test? It would certainly be much easier to justify the latter in terms of time and money required relative to information gained.

A number of different problems occur when an organization moves beyond testing specific abilities to either general aptitude or personality testing. These problems may include:

- Do the tests effectively screen for qualified applicants?

- Are any *qualified* job candidates eliminated from consideration on the basis of these tests? (This is an especially sensitive issue when female and minority candidates are involved.)

- Does the industry or organization have an ethical or legal right to "invade the privacy" of job applicants by asking highly personal questions (for example, those found on personality tests), especially if the questions do not seem to be directly related to an applicant's ability to do the job?

Because of these practical, ethical, and legal considerations, psychological testing in businesses and industries has markedly declined in recent years. One article (Tenopyr, 1981) reports the results of a survey conducted in 1975 by Prentice-Hall and the American Society for Personnel Administrators (ASPA) in which questionnaires were mailed to 2,000 ASPA member companies. The results of the survey indicate that 60 percent of the companies with 25,000 or more employees conducted at least some psychological testing, while 39 percent of the companies with fewer than 100 employees used psychological tests. One fourth of the total survey respondents said they limited testing to clerical job candidates.

Three fourths of the survey respondents indicated that they did less employee testing than they had done five years earlier. Fourteen percent said they planned to eliminate most psychological testing in the future. Tenopyr (1981) commented that "the legal requirements for testing are probably the primary cause of the decline in test use" (p. 1121). Interestingly, as Tenopyr points out, psychological tests may be the best, most valid, and most objective selection tools available. Yet because of the legal ramifications related to test usage, "the general reaction appears to be to flee from objective selection procedures rather than to attempt to comply with the guidelines" (p. 1121). Tenopyr goes on to say that psychological tests have been targeted by many groups as in need of validation; yet if employers do not use tests, their decisions may be based on interviews and letters of references—both of which (individually or together) are significantly less objective than psychological tests. So, as a result of legal and political pressures, organizations are making more personnel-related decisions without the most objective and valid information available. And if decisions are based more on variables such as education and experience, females and minorities may be at an even greater disadvantage than they are if test results are used.

Tenopyr is not alone in her statement that "a complete abandonment of employment testing and the substitution of alternatives, which are in many cases no more useful than a lottery for jobs, will not work to anyone's advantage in the long run" (p. 1125). D. P. Schultz (1978), while acknowledging that tests can be misused in the hands of unqualified individuals, suggests that employment testing is more economical and more objective than other selection processes. In a recent textbook, D. P. Schultz and S. E. Schultz (1986) paint a bleak picture based on the decline of psychological testing for personnel selection. "This rejection of sound psychological testing programs in personnel selection has had an unfortunate consequence on the economy in general. Because the right workers are not always being selected for the right jobs, the level of competence of the American work force has declined. This, in turn has led to a significant drop in worker productivity" (p. 124).

Assessment Centers   A fairly recent concept within the I/O field involves the use of so-called assessment centers to help in personnel selection and training. Assessment centers are not places where testing is conducted, as the name might indicate. Rather, they are multifaceted, standardized procedures involving a wide array of evaluation techniques, such as simulation and in-basket exercises.* Such procedures enable the I/O psychologist and others to observe a job candidate or trainee in one or more realistic settings and to assess the individual's ability to do the job and to work with others.

One of the challenges facing any business or organization is finding the best people for management-level positions. Individuals who are the most successful at nonmanagerial jobs do not necessarily make the most successful

---

* In-basket exercises are a type of simulation activity in which the person must deal with a pile of paperwork—letters, reports, phone messages, and so on—typical of what might be found in a manager's in-basket.

managers. Another example from the university setting may illustrate this point. The psychology department at a university is looking for a chairperson. Professors X, Y, and Z are possibilities. Professor X is a wonderful teacher. He is dynamic, informative, and humorous, always getting the highest teacher ratings in the department. Professor Y is the best-known researcher in the department. Her articles have been critically acclaimed and she has been awarded several large grants. Professor Z is a good teacher and researcher, but not necessarily outstanding in either category. On the other hand, Professor Z is organized and responsible. He is well liked by all of his colleagues and has a reputation for being fair and open-minded. Professors X and Y have each alienated a fair number of their colleagues by demanding special treatment. Professor X is known for his temper tantrums when things do not go his way, and Professor Y has difficulty remembering when and where her classes meet. Although Professors X and Y may be the most "successful" professors, Professor Z appears to possess better managerial characteristics than either of his colleagues and would probably be the best choice for the chairperson position.

The assessment center approach attempts to evaluate an individual's job-related strengths and weaknesses in a relatively standardized and efficient manner. A group of candidates for a particular type of job may be brought in for several days. During that time they participate in a series of simulated tasks similar to what they would be doing on-the-job. Observers rate and analyze their performances on these tasks. Assessment center experiences have been used increasingly since the 1960s; they seem to predict accurately variables such as supervisor's ratings and salary. The ability of assessment center performance to predict actual on-the-job performance has not been strongly substantiated.

Critics who question the fairness of the assessment center approach cite the subjectivity of the evaluation process—a candidate who is extremely qualified for a job but who is not charismatic may not score as well as the outgoing but minimally qualified applicant.

Training of Personnel

Once new employees have been recruited and selected, someone has to show them what they are expected to do. This may be a simple process of having a co-worker demonstrate the duties of the new job. At the other extreme, a large industry may hire several people at once for a particular position. A week or two of training sessions will orient the trainees to their new jobs and to the company for which they will be working. If the company is large enough, it may call upon the services of an I/O psychologist to:

1. Develop a training program based on job-analysis data.

2. Assess the skills of the trainees before training.

3. Plan and present a portion of the training to focus on psychological factors, such as attitudes, motivation, and coping with stress.

4. Observe the employees during training in an attempt to identify potential problems.

5. Evaluate the effectiveness of the training and the individual trainee's performance through a posttraining instrument.

Evaluating the effectiveness of the training (part 5) sounds easier than it is. The first step in evaluating a program may be to examine the desired outcome. If the goal is to orient new employees to the organization's policies and procedures, our method of evaluation will be far different than if the goal is to increase work performance and decrease employee turnover. The assessment technique in the first case might be a test geared to the employee's awareness of the policies and procedures. The second goal, however, would require long-term evaluation and follow-up of the group of trainees.

Ongoing Personnel Evaluation

Even though a student may come to college or graduate school with outstanding grades, glowing letters of recommendation, and the highest possible scores on the ACT, SAT, or GRE, he is not exempt from the ongoing evaluation process known as course grades. Why are grades given? Although there are people who would like to abandon the assignment of grades because they are unfair or counterproductive, most of us (faculty as well as students) view grades as at least somewhat useful and often necessary. Grades motivate students to complete their assignments; they give faculty a chance to reward hardworking students; and they provide students with feedback about their performance in a particular class. Grades can to a certain extent even provide faculty with feedback about their teaching, answering such questions as, Am I getting across to the students those concepts I consider most important? What topics should I emphasize?

On-the-job performance evaluations, in theory at least, serve the same functions. They give employees feedback, and they offer employers an opportunity to let hardworking employees know that they are doing well or to let not-so-hardworking employees know that they had better improve. Evaluations also provide valuable input to job analyses.

Again, though, these comments are theoretical. In reality, performance evaluations can be subjective, threatening, unfair, or even worthless. If administered fairly and seriously, they can be useful, providing the employer with the opportunity to reflect upon each individual's work—something that even the best managers may not always take the time to do. They can also provide the employees with feedback about their strengths as well as suggestions to improve their weaknesses. If not taken seriously, they may become another exercise in futility for the employee and the employer. Even worse, if administered unfairly, they may encourage favoritism or harassment in employers and discouragement, resentment, or anger in employees. If merit money or raises are based partially or totally on these evaluations, their relative importance increases significantly.

How can success on the job be measured? The answer depends on many factors, and this book cannot possibly elaborate on them all. Let us instead examine a few of the assessment-related issues involved in work performance evaluations and raise some critical questions.

Basis of Comparison

Should an employee be compared against some sort of absolute standard, compared against his or her co-workers, or both? A student takes a test and receives an "absolute" score of 80 percent. What does this tell us? Simply that out of every ten questions, he answered eight correctly. How would your opinion change if that 80 percent were the highest grade in the class? How about the lowest grade in the class? The basis of comparison can greatly influence the evaluation results.

Who Is Doing the Evaluating?

Any student of psychology must recognize the existence of individual differences and their impact on countless variables. Evaluation is certainly influenced by the person doing the evaluating, the person being evaluated, and the relationship between the two people.

Objective Measures of Performance

Are there any data that provide objective measures of occupational performance? L. Siegel and I. M. Lane (1982) suggest several such measures:

- *Productivity:* Counting the actual results of one's work.

- *Promotions and salary:* Has the employee been sufficiently successful to earn these tangible rewards?

- *Tenure and turnover:* How long has the individual been employed?

- *Miscellaneous:* Absences, illnesses, accidents, and so on.

None of these objective measures is above reproach. Productivity is rarely a viable measure, especially for the so-called white-collar jobs. Promotions and salary are confounded by the amount of movement within the organization, the amount of money available, and the method for its distribution. An organization may reward longevity (years of service) rather than actual job performance. Another problem with using promotion and salary as measures is that the initial decision to promote or to increase pay may have been subjective.

Tenure on the job can mean satisfaction or an inability to be hired elsewhere. The individual who is offered a better position in another organization may have been a far better employee than the individuals who were left behind.

Factors such as attendance or promptness do not automatically denote good performance. In my own college years I knew students who "studied all night" and obtained Ds while students who seemed to barely open their textbooks obtained Bs and As. Variables such as concentration, ability, motivation, alertness, and class attendance may have intervened. (I suppose cheating may have been a possibility in some cases as well.)

Surely, an I/O psychologist can play an important role in the development of employee evaluation measures as well as in the implementation of such scales. If I/O psychologists have access to these evaluations, they may be able to pinpoint difficulties that groups or individuals are having and attempt to correct these difficulties.

• • • • • •

EXAMPLE 5.1

THE I/O PSYCHOLOGIST IN A POLICE DEPARTMENT

P. is an industrial/organizational psychologist employed by the police department of a large metropolitan area. The police department's overall mission is to reduce and prevent criminal activities in the geographic area. The specific goals for 1988, as stated by the police department administration, include:

A. Responding more quickly to each call for assistance.

B. Offering a larger number of community service presentations about crime prevention.

C. Increasing the number of convictions for criminal activities.

P. might help the police department to achieve these goals through the examination of past practices. For goal A, responding more quickly to each call for assistance, P. would need to answer several questions:

• What was the average response time to calls in 1987?

• What were the range and distribution of the response times?

• Were the response times shorter during certain times of day (night versus day) or certain days of the week (Sunday versus Monday)?

- Were the response times shorter for particular sections of the city (lower income versus middle income)?

After collecting these data, P. might develop a survey to be completed by police officers and dispatchers asking for their observations regarding variations in response time and their suggestions for improvement. An analysis of such survey data could prove useful in pinpointing specific problem areas.

For goal B, offering a larger number of community service programs about crime prevention, P. would also need to collect data on past practices:

- How many such presentations were made in 1986?

- Were they effective (for example, were data collected from participants)?

- Who gave the presentations?

- Were the programs given only in response to a specific request from the public?

- How were topics decided?

- How many people attended the various programs?

At this point, P. might conduct a needs assessment of various community groups regarding their interest in such programs. In addition, P. might question police officers about their interest in making these presentations. If possible, P. might recruit a small group of police officers who seem to possess the interest, motivation, and abilities to make these presentations.

Goal C, increasing the number of convictions for criminal activities, also requires that P. scrutinize past practices:

- What have been the obstacles to convictions?

- What is the current arrest-to-conviction ratio?

- Do certain offenses seem to yield particularly low conviction rates?

P. might conclude from these investigations that more police officers are needed to meet goals A, B, and C. If the administration agrees with this recommendation, P. might be asked to help in the recruitment, selection, and training processes (as outlined earlier in this chapter). In addition, P. might be asked to suggest the allocation of work assignments of new and seasoned police officers.

What can P. do if the suggestion to hire more police officers is denied? There are at least three means of increasing the efficiency of the current staff:

1. Offer an incentive plan for improvement.

2. Modify current work assignments.

3. Provide a training program to teach more efficient practices.

The implementation of any or all of these ideas would ideally be based on the results of the needs assessments.

In all of these intervention plans, P. should conduct follow-up investigations to determine how the plans are working. P. would be well advised to assess not only if goals A, B, and C are being met but also how personnel feel about the changes. What problems have they encountered as a result of the new plan? What are the benefits of the new plan? What other services might P. offer as an I/O psychologist employed by a police department? The possibilities include:

- Stress management programs for police officers and their families.

- Suggestions for handling specific types of problems, such as domestic violence disputes, crimes by juveniles, hostage situations, child abuse/ neglect, potential suicides.

- Resolution of conflicts between partners.

- Treatment for substance abuse.

- Improvement of public relations.

- Prevention of burnout. •

• • • • • •

EXAMPLE 5.2

THE I/O PSYCHOLOGIST IN PRIVATE INDUSTRY

R. is an I/O psychologist who was recently hired by a large manufacturing firm. R.'s role centers upon personnel—the hiring, training, and evaluating of new employees. Although R. is the only I/O psychologist employed by the firm, several "personnel specialists" working for the firm conduct the reviews of applications and interviews with applicants. R. was hired for several reasons:

1. To assist the personnel department in keeping its hiring practices current with developments in I/O psychology.

2. To act as a liaison between the personnel department and the legal department in ensuring that all of the company's personnel policies are legal.

3. To oversee the training of new personnel.

4. To coordinate the company's annual employee evaluation program.

In her first month on the job, R. spent most of her time getting to know the people in the personnel department as well as the managers in the other departments currently recruiting employees. She reviewed the policies and procedures of the personnel department and found them somewhat outdated. In her interviews with personnel staff, she learned that the written policies were all but ignored.

R.'s next task was to rewrite and update the policies to conform with current psychological and legal principles. She placed special emphasis on the use of psychological testing in the interview process. R. recommended that Biodata Forms be used in the application process (as described earlier in this chapter, these forms are designed to facilitate the hiring of people who will stay with the organization and become successful employees). She also recommended that no personality testing be used and that interviewers complete a checklist at the conclusion of each interview rating the applicant on a variety of personal and professional characteristics. R. suggested that the tests of specific abilities needed in certain jobs (typing tests, tests of computer skills, and so on) be continued. She asked for a list of all of these tests and requested that personnel department employees keep records as to their frequency and their results.

R. scheduled a two-day meeting to introduce these new policies, to explain the rationale behind them, and to allow the employees a chance to practice filling out the new interview forms. After allowing time for feedback, R. found that a few of the new policy statements required further revisions for clarity.

Probably the most difficult task R. faced in her first year on the job was the coordination of the annual employee evaluation. Evaluations are always sensitive issues because they involve one person rating another. R. began by examining the current evaluation policies, interviewing several managers, and asking all employees to complete an anonymous survey. She found that the managers had few guidelines regarding employee evaluation and that the employees being evaluated felt that the evaluations were based more on personality (who the manager liked) than on work performance.

As with all psychological assessment practices, R. began her policy statement with a rationale—why are employees evaluated? She identified the following three reasons:

1. To maintain high levels of job performance.

2. To recognize outstanding employees.

3. To identify employees who are not working satisfactorily.

The current system required each manager to write a one-page description of each employee's job performance. R. recommended that a standardized checklist of behaviors be developed so that managers would not have to write lengthy accounts of each employee's performance. Under the new checklist system, each employee would be rated on a three-point scale (1 = exceptional, 2 = adequate, 3 = needs improvement) across a number of variables—from attitude and attendance to efficiency and skill. Some space would be left on the new form for optional comments.

R. suggested that managers keep careful records to document the "needs improvement" rating on any of the variables. She suggested further that managers meet individually with each employee to discuss that person's ratings and that both parties sign the evaluation form before sending it to the vice-president in charge of personnel. Employees would also be given the chance to file complaints about their evaluations. •

Ethical Considerations for the I/O Psychologist Using Psychological Assessment

In addition to the myriad of legal issues and controversies surrounding the usage of psychological assessment techniques for personnel decisions, I/O psychologists face a large number of professional and ethical controversies. M. London and D. W. Bray (1980) divide the ethical issues relevant to I/O psychologists into two major categories: the obligations of psychologists to their employers and the obligations of employers to the psychologists they employ. Psychologists' ethical responsibilities are further divided into their obligations to their profession, their obligations to job applicants and employees, and their obligations to their employers.

Of these ethical responsibilities, which relate most directly to the I/O psychologist's assessment-related functions?

- Psychologists must keep up to date in their profession. They must know which assessment techniques meet psychometric and legal standards for each particular set of circumstances and which assessment techniques are inappropriate.

- Psychologists must uphold the highest standards of professional conduct for themselves, and they must help to enforce these standards among their colleagues.

- Psychologists must protect the rights and privacy of the people with whom they work. They must respect the wishes of job applicants or employees and always operate with the "informed consent" of such individuals.

- Psychologists must provide their employers with the most accurate and highest quality information available.

The astute reader may have noticed that these last two principles may be in conflict at times. Such a conflict is not unique to the I/O psychologist. It raises the question of who the client is for the applied psychologist. Unfortunately, there is no clear-cut answer to this question. Industrial/organizational psychologists involved in personnel testing are responsible to their job applicants *and* to their employers. In an ideal world, the needs of these groups would not conflict. But conflicts do arise, and they are not always easy to resolve. For example, in the case of Example 5.1, (the I/O psychologist employed by a police department), P. has responsibilities to the administrators, the police officers, and the public. When conflicts arise, P. must use his best professional and ethical judgment to resolve them.

Other Uses of Assessment Techniques by I/O Psychologists

Personnel-related work is not the only domain in which I/O psychologists use psychological tests and other assessment techniques. I/O psychologists also use a variety of assessment techniques in the area of **marketing research**. These psychologists need to combine a knowledge of statistics, research methodology, and psychometric principles with large amounts of creativity and common sense to find out whether a particular product or service will succeed. Interest and attitude surveys are often used in such endeavors. I/O psychologists compare segments of the population in order to yield useful data. Advertising campaigns, which may be launched based on the results of these surveys, may in turn be subjected to testing by consumers. Marketing researchers are not always I/O psychologists, however. In fact, it is far more common to find applied statisticians or individuals with marketing degrees involved in marketing research than to find I/O psychologists in these positions.

Another area of interest to I/O psychologists that involves assessment procedures is called the **human factors** area. The human factors emphasis examines environmental impact on human functioning and seeks ways in which the environment can be modified to enhance functioning. Human factors research also focuses on workspace design and job design—for instance, do people work better under certain conditions of illumination, temperature, humidity, and noise level? The I/O psychologist interested in human factors examines these variables to determine their impact and suggests an optimal range under which the majority of people are most productive. Does painting the walls blue in an industrial setting facilitate performance? What about playing background music? Again, the I/O psychologist might examine the relationship between these variables and worker productivity or worker satisfaction.

What assessment techniques are useful in such research endeavors? The I/O psychologist would probably not administer IQ tests or personality measures to answer these questions. Instead, she might keep records of the work completed under different conditions. Observations made before and after an implemented change could determine the impact of the change. The I/O psychologist might ask workers for their opinions—either informally or through more formal channels such as structured interviews or questionnaires. Records of employee absentee rates or employee turnover might reveal relationships between those variables and the implemented change. (Of course, the I/O psychologist would have to be extremely cautious in interpreting any such results.)

A fourth area of interest to I/O psychologists is the organizational factors involved when a group of people work together. If we think of personnel work as getting the right person in the right job, marketing work as putting out a successful product, and human factors work as modifying the environment to suit the person, then we can think of **organizational psychology** as concerned with human behavior within an organization or group.

Businesses, industries, and other organizations ideally are composed of individuals working together for a common goal. Organizational specialists examine such variables as worker satisfaction, leadership skills, styles of management, intergroup communication, and conflict resolution. As in marketing and human factors research, the I/O psychologist specializing in organizational behavior uses a variety of assessment procedures to accomplish specific goals. Traditional, individually administered psychological tests would probably not be as useful as observational techniques, questionnaires, and interviews.

Concluding Remarks

Although all four of the areas mentioned in this chapter are worth considering, most of the chapter has been devoted to personnel selection and classification. The reason for this emphasis is simply that the area of personnel selection and classification is the area of I/O psychology that is most intimately tied to traditional psychological assessment techniques. Readers interested in other I/O specialties should pursue their interests through course work and readings.*

I/O psychologists use a wide variety of assessment procedures in their work, several of which have been described in this chapter. I/O psychology is currently undergoing a tremendous increase in popularity. It seems likely that the use of assessment procedures in I/O psychology will enjoy a similar increase in popularity.

ADDITIONAL READING

For more information about industrial/organizational psychology, consult the following sources.

Recent Books

Dunnette, M. (Ed.). (1976). *Handbook of industrial and organizational psychology.* Chicago: Rand McNally.
Huchingson, R. D. (1981). *New horizons for human factors in design.* New York: McGraw-Hill.

---

* The list of books and journals at the end of this chapter suggests additional information for the other areas of industrial/organizational psychology.

Huse, E. F. (1980). *Organization development and change.* St. Paul, MN: West.

Katzell, R. A., Yankelovich, D., Fein, M., Ornati, D. A., & Nash, A. (1975). *Work, productivity and job satisfaction.* New York: Psychological Corporation.

Klein, S. M., & Ritti, R. R. (1980). *Understanding organizational behaviors.* Boston: Kent.

Landy, F. J. (1985). *Psychology of work behavior* (3rd. ed.). Homewood, IL: Dorsey Press.

Latham, G. P., & Wexley, K. N. (1981). *Increasing productivity through performance appraisal.* Reading, MA: Addison-Wesley.

Leavitt, H. J. (1978). *Managerial psychology* (4th ed.). Chicago: University of Chicago Press.

McCormick, E. J., & Sanders, M. S. (1982). *Human factors in engineering and design* (5th ed.). New York: McGraw-Hill.

Miller, K. M. (Ed.). (1975). *Psychological testing in personnel assessment.* New York: John Wiley and Sons.

Miner, J. B. (1980). *Theories of organizational behavior.* Hinsdale, IL: Dryden Press.

Mowday, R. T., Porter, L. W., & Steers, R. M. (1982). *Employee-organizational linkages: The psychology of commitment, absenteeism, and turnover.* New York: Academic Press.

Schiffman, L. G., & Kanuk, L. K. (1983). *Consumer behavior* (2nd ed.). Englewood Cliffs, NJ: Prentice-Hall.

Schultz, D. P., & Schultz, S. E. (1986). *Psychology and industry today* (4th ed.). New York: Macmillan.

Siegel, L., & Lane, I. M. (1982). *Personnel and organizational psychology.* Homewood, IL: Richard D. Irwin.

Woods, W. A. (1981). *Consumer behavior: Adapting and experiencing.* New York: Elsevier.

Journals

The Industrial-Organizational Psychologist
Industrial Psychology
Journal of Applied Psychology
Journal of Occupational Psychology
Journal of Vocational Behavior
Organizational Behavior and Human Decision Processes
Personnel Psychology

C H A P T E R 6

Psychological Assessment and the School Psychologist

Perhaps more than any of the other applied areas of psychology, school psychology has been closely associated with psychological testing and assessment. Surveys of school psychologists indicate that the majority of their time is devoted to assessment-related activities. This chapter will describe some of the ways in which school psychologists use psychological tests and other assessment procedures.

Preschool Screening

A group of three- and four-year-olds enters a large room. It is preschool screening week. Some of the children are smiling; others are crying. Some are holding their mothers' hands; others have just arrived en masse from their preschool rooms and day-care centers. Some can read already; others are just starting to identify colors.

School psychologists use preschool assessment for *prevention*—they try to detect difficulties and remedy them as early as possible. If a child with a learning difficulty spends a year or two in school before the difficulty is identified, the chances are good that a sense of frustration will start to build. Some children cope with frustration by exhibiting a wide array of inappropriate behaviors. Other children are convinced that there is something wrong with them—they must be awfully "dumb" if they cannot learn to read as well as their classmates. These children may withdraw from the situation, not wanting to call attention to themselves or their problems. Either way, the learning difficulty is compounded with a behavioral or emotional difficulty that makes the problem worse.

If children who are likely to exhibit learning difficulties can be identified prior to school entrance, however, intervention efforts can begin before the child experiences frustration and self-doubts. In some cases, the child can be enrolled in a school district's preschool program in order to receive professional assistance. In other, less severe, cases, parents may receive lists of suggested activities that they can do with their child at home. For example, parents of a three-year-old who would not follow directions during preschool screening might receive the following list of suggestions:

1. Have your child's hearing checked by your pediatrician.

2. Give simple directions to your child, using words such as *under, over, next to, on top of,* and so on. For example, "Put this yellow pencil under the kitchen table."

3. Start out with one direction at a time, and gradually increase to two and then three. For example, "Put the book on the blue chair, bring me the pencil from the kitchen table, then come back and sit down on the sofa."

4. Praise your child when he or she does follow directions.

5. Always make sure you have your child's attention before you start giving your instructions.

With suggestions such as these for parents and placement in a preschool setting, the child may not have a problem by the time she or he is ready to start school. Preschool screening is also beneficial for children who have no major difficulties, as it can be reassuring for parents to know that their children are developing normally. Also, since parents often attend the screenings with their child, they are able to observe their child's reactions to a variety of experiences, and they may get some ideas for activities to try at home as well.

The school psychologist's role in preschool screening activities is not uniform across school districts. In small school districts the school psychologist might be in charge of choosing the test instrument for the screening and "running the show." In medium-sized districts the psychologist might be responsible for administering certain parts of the test and setting the standards for passing the test. In large districts the school psychologist might be called upon only to "rescreen" or follow up on those children who experienced difficulty with the screening.

Although historically school psychologists have not typically worked with the preschool-age population, there has been a great deal of movement in that direction, particularly for youngsters identified as disabled or deemed to be "at risk" to develop school-related problems—that is, premature, low birth rate, and low socioeconomic status children. The current thinking seems to be that if a problem is likely to develop, children, parents, and school personnel are better off if it can be alleviated or lessened as early as possible. School districts have developed programs for preschoolers, and the school psychologist, along with other members of the pupil personnel services team (social worker, speech therapist, and special education teachers), is responsible for identifying, assessing, and placing children in these programs. The preschool screening provides one opportunity to identify youngsters who are at risk. In other cases, parents, other family members, or community agency personnel may alert the school district to a child who is experiencing difficulties. Assessment of preschoolers usually entails examining the child's language development, fine and gross motor development, social and emotional development, physical development, and development of self-help skills (feeding, dressing, and so forth).

School-Aged Children

Once children enter school, the testing-related responsibilities of the school psychologist tend to be more uniform. When a child is having difficulty in school, the school psychologist is usually called upon to provide insights into the reasons for the difficulty and to offer suggestions that might help correct it. Since the passage of Public Law 94-142 in 1975, school districts across the country have been required to identify, diagnose, and provide appropriate educational services to all handicapped children. The term *handicapped* includes a wide range of disabilities, from the child in need of some speech and language services to the "low-incidence" (that is, visually impaired, hearing impaired, or physically disabled) child. (Table 6.1 outlines the major concepts of Public Law 94-142.) In order to comply with P.L. 94-142, most school psychologists spend a large amount of time consulting with school personnel and with parents to meet the needs of handicapped youngsters.

Much of the school psychologist's role in this process centers around the use of assessment techniques to identify children in need of special education services and to diagnose each child's particular strengths and weaknesses. The following outline illustrates the school psychologist's role in the identification, diagnostic, and placement process.

Step 1: Referral

A child (or adolescent) is referred to the school psychologist by a teacher, parent, or other concerned person, such as a school principal or physician. The individual making the referral completes a referral form, which generally includes information similar to the sample provided in Table 6.2.

T A B L E 6.1 Summary of Major Concepts of Public Law 94-142

Free Appropriate Public Education for all Handicapped Children

All handicapped children are entitled to a free, public education appropriate to their needs and abilities.

Nondiscriminatory Evaluation Procedures

In order to qualify for special services, the child must be evaluated by trained personnel. The assessment procedures must be administered in a standardized manner in the child's native language. No single test or other assessment technique may be used as the sole criterion for identification and placement. The evaluation should include assessments of all areas that might relate to the child's disability, including some or all of the following: health, vision, hearing, social and emotional functioning, overall intelligence, academic achievement, motor abilities, and competence in communication.

Individualized Education Programs

Trained personnel should prepare a written statement of services provided, including educational goals and objectives for each handicapped child.

T A B L E 6.2 Mike's Referral for Evaluation

  I. Personal Information

      Name of child: **Mike A.**   Date of request: **1/27/87**
      Address: **123 Oak Lane**   Date of birth: **5/27/80**
      Home telephone: **837-1910** Age: **6 years, 8 months**

 II. Family Information
      Name   Education   Occupation
      Father: **Richard A.**   **H. S. grad Construction foreman**
      Mother: **Millicent A.**   **H. S. grad Police officer**
      Ages of siblings: **10, 13**
      Is this child ___ adopted or stepchild
                     ___ foster child
                     _X_ living with only one parent
      Primary language of home: _X_ English ___ Other (specify)

III. School Information

      Name of school: **James Elementary School**
      Address: **2001 Skinner St.**
      Telephone: **837-1155**   Principal: **Mr. Ed Grant**
      Child's present grade: 1 Teacher: **Ms. P. Etta**
      Grades repeated: **none**   Years in present school: **1$^1/_2$**
      Services presently offered to the child: **none**
      Attendance record: **good; missed 4 days so far this year**
      Previous schools attended: **none**

Least Restrictive Environment

Every effort should be made for handicapped children to be educated with nonhandicapped children. Handicapped children should be "mainstreamed" into regular educational classes and activities as much as possible.

Due Process

The due process procedures of P.L. 94-142 emphasize the rights and the responsi-bilities of all parties involved in the identification, diagnosis, and placement of handicapped children. Specific steps are detailed when disagreements arise between the parents and the school system.

Parental Participation

P.L. 94-142 emphasizes the rights of parents to be involved in their children's education. Parents must be kept informed of every step in their children's identifi-cation, diagnosis, and placement procedures. Parents should become active participants in deciding the best options for their children's needs.

IV. Health Information

    Date of last physical examination: **8/29/86**
    Name of doctor: **Arnold Fried**
    Is this child on medication? **no**   If so, what?_____
    Date and results of last vision screening: **9/10/86 OK**
    Date and results of last hearing test: **9/10/86 OK**
    General physical health: **good**
    During the last year has the child experienced any medical problems? If yes, please explain.
    2 colds
    stomach flu once

V. Reason for Referral

    A. Why are you referring this child for psychological evaluation? What questions would you like to have answered?
    Mike can't keep up with the rest of the class. He has good days and bad days. I want to know what his prob-lem is and whether he needs tutoring or special class placement.

    B. Is there anything about the child's home or family environment that you believe might have a bearing on the child's attitude and behavior? If so, please explain.
    Parents recently separated. Mike greatly misses his father.

Step 2: Clarification of Referral Problem

Clarification of the referral problem involves addressing questions such as: What is the presenting problem? Why was the assessment requested? Is there an answerable referral question?

To clarify the problem, the school psychologist may wish to contact and interview the child, the parent(s), the teacher(s), and any other potential sources of information.

Step 3: Formation of Initial Hypotheses

In this step the school psychologist starts to develop hypotheses about what the difficulty may be and what additional information is needed to substantiate or refute these hypotheses. This is probably the most difficult step for school psychology students and interns because such hypotheses tend to be educated hunches based on at least a limited amount of experience.

Step 4: Data Gathering, Including Test Selection, Administration, and Scoring

This step encompasses many different processes. For example, in order to gather all of the necessary information about a particular child, the school psychologist may perform some or all of the following activities:

I. Parent interview:

　　A. Health history/developmental history
　　　　1. Information related to pregnancy and birth— for example were there any complications with the pregnancy and birth?
　　　　2. Information related to developmental tasks, such as when did the child master each of the following:
　　　　　　a. Sitting
　　　　　　b. Crawling
　　　　　　c. Standing
　　　　　　d. Walking
　　　　　　e. Talking
　　　　　　f. Toilet training
　　　　3. Information about childhood illnesses, accidents, and hospitalizations—what kinds and how often?
　　　　4. How is the child's school attendance record?
　　　　5. What were the results of the child's most recent physical exam and vision and hearing screenings?

B. Family background and status
 1. Names and ages of siblings
     a. Their grade(s) in school
     b. Their level(s) of achievement
     c. Sibling relationships in the family
 2. Significant events
     a. Adoption
     b. Parental absence or separation
     c. Divorce
     d. Death
     e. Others living in the home
     f. Employment status of both parents
 3. Family rules
     a. Discipline used and its effectiveness
     b. Bedtimes, mealtimes, and other routines
     c. Rewards and punishments
     d. Responsibilities/chores
 4. Parent-child relationship
 5. Family activities and plans
 6. Child's behavior at home and in the neighborhood
 7. Primary language spoken in the home

C. Parental attitudes
 1. Parents' educational background
 2. Parents' cooperation with the school
 3. Do the parents believe that a problem exists?
 4. What do the parents think has caused the problem?
 5. From the parents' perspective, what has been done, or should be done, to alleviate the problem?
 6. Parents' desired outcome of assessment
 7. Parents' aspirations for the child (for example, college)
 8. Parents' level of commitment to cooperate in interventions

II. Examination of school records

 A. Current grade placement

 B. Has the child ever been retained or accelerated? Has the child received any kind of special services?

 C. Group test results

 D. Attendance record

 E. Previous psychological reports—has the child worked with a psychologist before? If so, what clues do previous reports provide about the problem and its resolution?

III. Teacher interview

    A. Why was the child referred?

    B. What are the child's strengths and weaknesses in:
        1. Academic areas
        2. Behavior (in specific terms)
        3. Attitude
        4. Peer relationships

    C. In-class behavior

    D. Teacher's expectations for the child

    E. Teacher's expectations of assessment results

    F. What remediation techniques has the teacher already tried to implement?
        1. What was done?
        2. How long did they last?
        3. What happened?

    G. How long has the teacher been teaching? What grades? Where?

    H. Number of referrals received from this teacher

    I. How cooperative will the teacher be in participating in classroom interventions?

IV. Classroom observations

    A. What was the child supposed to be doing?

    B. What was the child doing? What were the other children doing?

    C. What sort of observation occurred?
        1. Systematic (a formal observation technique)
        2. Nonsystematic (a "global observation"—sitting and watching what the child is doing)

    D. Where did you observe? (class, playground, lunchroom)

    E. When and for how long did you observe?

    F. What led up to and what were the consequences of the child's behavior?

    G. How did you know whom to observe?

    H. Did the child seem to know he or she was being observed?

    I. Did the observation provide you with any clues about the problem and its resolution?

V. Testing

    A. What do you want to know?

    B. What tests can best provide you with that information?

C. Are the tests appropriate for the child's age, ethnic background, educational history, and so on?

D. How did you establish rapport?

E. How did the child seem to enjoy the testing?

F. Does the child know why the testing took place?

G. What does the child see as his or her strengths and weaknesses?

H. Behavior during testing (give concrete examples):
   1. Impulsive/reflective
   2. Talkative/reticent
   3. Attention span
   4. Were rewards needed as motivation?
   5. Diversionary tactics (did the child try to change the subject?)
   6. Quality of verbalizations (sentence length,vocabulary used)

I. Conditions during testing
   1. Was the child concerned about what she or he was missing in the classroom?
   2. Was the child in good health and rested?
   3. When was the testing done?
      a. How many sessions?
      b. How long?
      c. Morning or afternoon?
   4. Where was the testing done?
   5. What distractions were present?

J. Other observations
   1. Is the child right-handed or left-handed?
   2. How closely did he or she hold the paper while reading or writing?

Step 5: Interpretation of Data and Modification of Initial Hypotheses

Based on all of the data collected:

1. What are the child's strengths and weaknesses?

2. What seems to be the problem?

3. What has aggravated the problem so that the child was referred at this time?

4. Is any additional information needed?

Step 6: Communication of Results

1. Synthesizing the information in a written report.

2. Communicating information orally with parents, teachers, and others.

    a. Present specific findings.
    b. Generate alternative solutions in cooperation with parents and school personnel.

Step 7: Implementation of Recommendations

The school psychologist often implements recommendations indirectly, acting as a consultant to teachers and parents.

Step 8: Follow-up and Evaluation

1. Were we correct in our diagnosis?

2. Are the recommendations working?

3. What can be done to improve the situation further?

These are the steps that school psychologists follow in conducting assessments. The following examples illustrate this process.

● ● ● ● ● ●

EXAMPLE 6.1

MIKE

A school psychologist receives a referral from a first-grade teacher regarding a six-year-old boy who is "unable to keep up with the rest of the class" (Table 6.2). The teacher wants to know what the problem is and whether the child should be receiving some special services.

The psychologist, seeking to clarify the problem, consults with the boy's parents and his teacher, checks the boy's permanent record, and observes the youngster in the classroom and out on the playground. The following are the results of these procedures:

Mike is a six-year-old boy who is having difficulty paying attention and completing his work in the first-grade classroom. His teacher reports that especially since Thanksgiving, Mike seems to have "good days and bad days." On his "good" days he can identify most letters and the sounds they make. He seems eager to please his teacher. On his "bad" days he confuses letters and numbers and seems to be "in a world of his own." Mike's mother, Mrs. A., has observed similar behavior patterns in Mike at home. At times he is delighted to help her with chores around the house; at other times he sits listlessly in front of the TV set for hours. On these "bad" days, Mike has to be prodded and reminded to follow even the simplest directions. Mrs. A. reported that Mike sometimes has difficulty falling asleep, and at other times he sleeps restlessly, tossing and turning a great deal. Mrs. A. said that she and Mr. A. have been having marital difficulties recently and that Mike seems upset by the frequent arguments. Mr. A. moved out of the home one month ago for a "trial separation." Mrs. A. said that Mike and his father have always been particularly close and that his listless and in-attentive behavior has increased since Mr. A.'s departure.

Mike's school records indicate that he had no difficulties in kindergarten. He was described as a "happy, well-rounded youngster."

At this point the school psychologist hypothesizes that Mike's school diffi-culties are not a result of any lack of intellectual ability but rather that they stem from a crisis reaction to events occurring in the home. The psychologist selects several test instruments to administer to Mike. She wants to test Mike for three reasons: first, to double-check whether he does have the ability to perform the work expected of him; second, to provide her with a relatively standardized setting in which to observe Mike's behavior and reactions; and third, to investi-gate whether Mike's distress over his parents' separation is indeed having a negative effect on his schoolwork. The tests include the Wechsler Intelligence Scale for Children—Revised (WISC-R) to measure overall ability and the achieve-ment portions of the Woodcock-Johnson Psychoeducational Battery to measure academic progress. In addition, the psychologist asks Mrs. A. to complete the Personality Inventory for Children (PIC), a test that consists of twelve clinical scales and three validity scales. Finally, the psychologist selects a sentence com-pletion inventory to use with Mike as a means of questioning him about his feelings. After preparing the room where testing will take place to minimize the number of potential distractions, the school psychologist goes to Mike's class-room and asks Mike to come with her.

As the psychologist walks Mike to the testing room and as they enter the room, she concentrates on the rapport-building process. If Mike seems appre-hensive, she will probably say something to reassure him.

SCHOOL PSYCHOLOGIST: I think you'll enjoy some of the activities we'll be doing this morning. I will be asking you some questions, having you put some puzzles together, and asking you to figure out some pictures. I want to see what you are good at and what you have difficulty with so I can help you to do your best at school. What do you think is the thing you do the best?

MIKE: I'm a good swimmer, and I'm good at baseball.

S.P.: Is there anything you can think of that you have trouble with?

MIKE: Mom says I have trouble paying attention.

S.P.: Do you think she's right?

MIKE: I guess so. I lose my place a lot in school, and when my mom asks me to do something at home, I usually forget and she gets mad.

S.P.: What is your best subject in school?

MIKE: I like arithmetic pretty well.

S.P.: What do you have trouble with at school?

MIKE: I can't read as well as the other kids in my class.

S.P.: How does that make you feel?

MIKE: Dumb!

S.P.: How about if we start working on some of the things I have here, and I'll see if I can help you read better.

MIKE: I guess so.

Because the psychologist feels that Mike is fairly comfortable with her now and has a general understanding of the purpose of the testing, she begins to administer the Wechsler Intelligence Scale for Children—Revised (WISC-R). This test takes about one hour, and the psychologist notices that toward the end of the testing, Mike is restless and showing signs of fatigue. She concludes testing for the day and promises that they will finish later the same week. During the second session she administers the remainder of the test instruments and thanks Mike for being such a good worker.

After scoring the tests, the school psychologist summarizes the results as follows:

On the Wechsler Intelligence Scale for Children—Revised (WISC-R), Mike scored in the bright-normal range (110–120) for Verbal IQ, Performance IQ, and Full Scale IQ. His performance was fairly consistent across all subtests.

On the achievement portion of the Woodcock-Johnson Psychoeducational Battery, Mike scored as follows:

	Percentile Rank	Standard Score (mean 100)
Reading Cluster	17	86
Math Cluster	81	113
Written Language Cluster	12	82
Knowledge	93	122

He clearly demonstrated significant weaknesses in reading and written language, but his math and knowledge skills seemed quite strong. These scores closely match the observations of Mike's teacher and mother. Mike was not able to sound out words. Instead, he looked at the first letter and then guessed.

Throughout the testing, Mike made comments that seemed to indicate a low self-image. He frequently said, "That's too hard for me. . . . I can't do that" and similar remarks. On the Personality Inventory for Children (PIC), Mike's mother indicated that Mike's family life is unstable (with his parents' recent separation) and that Mike is somewhat anxious and withdrawn.

Mike seemed to enjoy the testing, and he put forth a great deal of effort on all of the tasks presented to him. He was careful in his work and would usually think for a while before answering. The exception to his careful work habits occurred when he was asked to read. On reading tasks he seemed to say aloud the first word that came to his mind. •

Now that the school psychologist has reported the specific test results and observed behaviors, it is time to pull the information together and make recommendations. In Mike's case, this section might read as follows:

Based on the testing and observations reported above, two areas seem to need attention. The first area involves Mike's reading skills. The following suggestions might prove helpful in developing Mike's ability in reading:

1. Provide an opportunity for small groups or, if possible, individualized help for Mike in reading.

2. Help Mike develop phonics (sounding out) skills as he attacks new words.

3. Encourage Mike to use contextual clues (that is, pictures and the other words in the sentence) when he comes to an unfamiliar word.

The second area of concern is Mike's low self-esteem. His parents' recent separation and his difficulty with reading seem to be having a negative impact on his feelings about himself. Suggestions to enhance Mike's self-esteem include:

1. Start at instructional levels in school at which Mike can be guaranteed success.

2. Introduce new words and skills gradually, always including some opportunities for success.

3. Praise Mike for attempts as well as actual successes at home and at school.

4. Talk to Mike about the separation, emphasizing that he is not to blame and that whatever the outcome is, he is loved. Also, there are numerous books written for children about separation and divorce. Take the time to read and talk about one or more such books with Mike.

5.   Consider giving Mike a special responsibility at home and at school, such as feeding the fish or watering the plants. This may help him feel special and important.

At this point the psychologist talks to Mike's parents, teachers, and others about her findings and recommendations. Because of the possibility of placement in a special education resource room, in this case a program for learning-disabled students, the sharing of the results of assessment probably takes place at a multidisciplinary staff conference. The meeting brings together all the people who have worked with Mike or who will play a role in his education—Mike's parents, his teacher, the school psychologist, the school principal, the school social worker (when applicable), and the learning disabilities teacher. As a group, the members of this multidisciplinary team describe Mike's current levels of functioning, his strengths and his weaknesses, and the areas of concern. Following the presentation of this information, a consensus is reached as to what special education services, if any, Mike will receive and what the short- and long-term goals of such services are.

In Mike's case, based on the results of testing, the school psychologist and others at the staff conference decide that Mike should receive individual help from the special education resource room teacher twenty minutes a day, five days a week. The resource room teacher will help develop Mike's reading skills, using a combination of phonics and the sight word approach. The resource room teacher will consult at least once a week with Mike's regular classroom teacher to monitor his progress and to work on particular problem areas as they arise. The long-term goal of the resource room is to bring Mike's reading up to the late first-grade level by the end of the school year. The members of the multidisciplinary team emphasize that praise for specific behaviors (for example, "I like the way you read that whole page to me") should be used generously at school and at home in order to raise Mike's self-esteem.

After the staff conference, the group completes a written report of the results of the entire assessment process. This report becomes part of Mike's school record. Even though Mike is only six, the school psychologist may meet with him and tell him how well he did and how much she enjoyed working with him. She may provide Mike with specific information about his strengths and weaknesses using language and concepts that are appropriate to his age.

In May, the school psychologist checked up on Mike's progress. She found that Mike had made great progress in reading with the help of the resource teacher, that he was reading at the late first-grade reading level (the long-term goal), and that he was much happier in his schoolwork and at home. Mike's resource room teacher used a **Curriculum-Based Assessment (CBA) system** to monitor Mike's academic progress. The CBA system assesses each student in a specific instructional content area. In Mike's case, the resource room teacher tested his ability to read aloud from the reading series used in his classroom. She also tested his comprehension of the material. Based on the results of these tests, Mike's teacher discovered that Mike had mastered the so-called prereading skills and was ready for the basic concepts of reading. Mike learned quickly and helped his teacher keep a chart to measure his weekly progress. The chart and his newly acquired reading skills not only increased his motivation to read but also had a positive impact on his self-esteem. Mike's regular classroom teacher and his parents reported that Mike was smiling more and seemed happier. Mike's resource room teacher agreed to tutor Mike twice a week over the summer to ensure his continued progress. In addition, Mike's parents are working on a reconciliation and are attending marriage counseling sessions. •

• • • • • •

EXAMPLE 6.2

TABITHA

In May, a school psychologist attends a meeting with the junior high school principal and the mother of a child who will start junior high in the fall. The mother has just bought a home and will move into the school district over the summer. At the meeting the mother explains her concerns:

Tabitha is thirteen years old and a very smart child. In her last school she was in a special class for the disabled because she has cerebral palsy. She walks with great difficulty and usually uses a wheelchair to get around in school. Her speech is hard to understand, and she cannot write legibly. I would like for her to be in "regular" classes because she needs the intellectual and social stimulation of "normal kids." I wanted to let you know right away because in all likelihood, some special arrangements will have to be made. I have a copy of her previous psychological report, but it is three years old, and I would like to have some new testing done—over the summer, if possible. I think that the speech therapist should also do some testing at this time.

At this initial meeting the school psychologist gives Tabitha's mother a referral form to complete and a parental permission form to sign. Parental permission is vital when psychological assessments are conducted with children. It keeps the parents apprised of the assessment process and gives them the opportunity to air their concerns. The vast majority of parents want their children to succeed in and out of school. Often they are the first to notice their children's difficulties, and in many cases the parents initiate the referral process. In addition, because parental permission is legally required, school psychologists are taking an unnecessary risk in proceeding with an assessment procedure prior to obtaining informed consent from a child's parent or guardian. The term *informed consent* means that the entire assessment process, including the reasons for assessment and the possible outcomes, should be explained to the parents in a comprehensible manner. The school psychologist should use as little technical jargon as possible. If the parents do not speak English, a translator should be hired to interpret the information.

Judging from her introductory statement, Tabitha's mother appears to be aware of the assessment process. Also, because she requested the testing, a lengthy explanation of the reasons for and process of assessment is probably not necessary. Because Tabitha's mother is eager for the testing to begin, she quickly signs the permission form and promises to complete the referral form and bring it in the next day. She also leaves a copy of Tabitha's previous psychological report with the psychologist and sets up a mutually convenient time with the school psychologist to begin testing .

After reading the referral form (Table 6.3) and the previous psychological report, the school psychologist chooses the appropriate test instruments to use. The school psychologist asks the speech therapist for some assistance in the assessment process because of the mother's report that Tabitha's speech is hard to understand.

The results of the previous psychological report (conducted three and a half years earlier, when Tabitha was nine years old) can be summarized as follows:

Tabitha is a sweet and cooperative child. She enjoys being challenged and seems very bright. Her speech is difficult to understand, but she seems to comprehend everything said to her. Because of her speech and her motor impairments, the typical sorts of tests could not be administered. She was able to point to the answer on the Peabody Picture Vocabulary Test, and on that test she obtained an IQ equivalent of 130, placing her in the superior-to-gifted range of ability. Based on her disabling conditions, the multidisciplinary team met and recommended that Tabitha be placed full-time in the class for low-incidence handicapped children.

Following the conference with Tabitha's mother and the results of the previous report, the school psychologist decides to administer the Columbia Mental Maturity Scale, the Peabody Picture Vocabulary Test—Revised (PPVT-R), and the Peabody Individual Achievement Test. None of these tests requires speech or motor skills. Usually, in all three the test taker is asked to point to the correct answer or to tell the examiner the number of the square in which the correct answer is found. All three instruments, however, can be easily adapted to a variety of disabilities. For example, the examiner can point to all of the squares and the child merely has to nod to choose one, or the child can hold up the correct number of fingers.

In addition, the psychologist administers the American Association on Mental Deficiency's (AAMD) Adaptive Behavior Scale, Public School Version—Revised to Tabitha and her mother. The scale is a structured interview that examines a child's skills in nonacademic areas. There are questions about eating habits (for example, using forks and knives), dressing (can the child dress herself ?) use of the telephone, ability to tell time, and so forth. The school psychologist may use the scale to decide what special arrangements are necessary if Tabitha is placed in a regular classroom. The AAMD Adaptive Behavior Scale also assesses social skills.

Finally, in preparing to test Tabitha, the school psychologist asks Tabitha's mother to send a copy of Tabitha's previous school records and a report from

T A B L E 6.3 Tabitha's Referral for Evaluation

I. Personal Information
    Name of child: **Tabitha B.** Date of request: **5/27/87**
    Address: **11 Martin Lane** Date of birth: **4/23/74**
    Home telephone: **836-2020** Age: **13 years, 1 month**

II. Family Information

    Name   Education   Occupation
    Father: **Michael B.**   **College grad** **Book salesman**
    Mother: **Samantha B.**   **College grad** **Librarian**
    Ages of siblings: **none**
    Is this child ___ adopted or stepchild
                  ___ foster child
                   X_ living with only one parent
    Primary language of home: X_ English ___ Other (specify)

III. School Information

    Name of school: **Eleanor Roosevelt Junior High School**
    Address: **100 Washington Ave.**
    Telephone: **837-1919**   Principal: **Mr. Pat Brooks**
    Child's present grade: **7** Teacher: **(previous)**
                                            Mrs. W. Nance
    Grades repeated: **none**   Years in present school: **none**
    Services presently offered to the child: **special class**
    Attendance record: **fair, missed 3 weeks last year**
    Previous schools attended: **two (elementary school)**

IV. Health Information

    Date of last physical examination: **9/10/86**
    Name of doctor: **B. Green**
    Is this child on medication? **no**   If so, what?_____
    Date and results of last vision screening: **8/29/85 OK**
    Date and results of last hearing test: **5/27/84 OK**
    General physical health: **See physician's report.**
    During the last year has the child experienced any medi-
    cal problems? If yes, please explain.
    pneumonia (missed 2 weeks of school)
    stomach flu twice

V. Reason for Referral

    A. Why are you referring this child for psychological
    evaluation? What questions would you like to have answered?
    We have just moved to this school district. Tabitha has
    cerebral palsy. She will need some support services to

Continued

TABLE 6.3 Continued

function in a regular classroom. Her mobility is limited, and her speech is hard to understand. She also has great difficulty writing legibly. Her typing skills are coming along, but her motor impairments get in the way.

I want to know if Tabitha can function in a regular classroom. If so, what kinds of services are available to assist her? Also, she needs to work on learning to like herself and on getting along with her classmates, especially boys. Can something be done in that area?

B. Is there anything about the child's home or family environment that you believe might have a bearing on the child's attitude and behavior? If so, please explain.

Tabitha's father and I are divorced and have been for ten years. He had a difficult time accepting that his child was disabled. He pays child support but doesn't seem comfortable spending time with Tabitha. Because Tabitha is an only child with no males around at home, she feels extremely uncomfortable in the company of boys and men. I date infrequently, but when I do, Tabitha becomes very upset and withdrawn. Now that she's a teenager I'm especially concerned about this attitude.

Tabitha's physician. These reports will help the new school system to understand more about the **etiology,** or causes, of Tabitha's cerebral palsy and about her ability to function within a school environment.

After completing the data collection and testing phase of the assessment process, a multidisciplinary staff conference occurs. Those present at the conference include Tabitha's mother, the school psychologist, the building principal, the guidance counselor, the speech therapist, the school nurse, and several seventh-grade teachers. The participants make the following recommendations:

1. Tabitha will be enrolled in "regular" seventh-grade classes.

2. A full-time aide will be employed to accompany Tabitha throughout the day to help her between classes.

3. Tabitha will receive speech therapy three times a week.

4. Tabitha will receive physical therapy twice a week.

5. After the first four weeks of school, Tabitha and her mother will meet with school personnel to discuss any concerns.

6. Tabitha's teachers will work together to develop ways to assess her academic progress. Their efforts will be described at the follow-up meeting.

Several issues were aired at the follow-up meeting. Tabitha had progressed academically. The teachers tested her orally over material covered. Their efforts were most successful when an aide or speech therapist "translated" words that the teachers could not understand.

Tabitha's social development still needed improvement—her classmates were ignoring her, and she continued to have difficulty relating to males. The participants suggested several ideas for improving the situation. An aide would still be used most of the time, but two or three of Tabitha's classmates (boys and girls) would take turns helping Tabitha get to her first two classes every day. In addition, the male guidance counselor volunteered to lead a small group (perhaps five or six girls including Tabitha) once a week to discuss their feelings about a variety of issues. The group might help all of the girls discover their strengths and similarities. Finally, Tabitha should be assigned to classes with male teachers whenever possible.

The multidisciplinary team met again prior to Thanksgiving to monitor Tabitha's progress. The group found that Tabitha had continued to progress in her schoolwork and that she felt much more comfortable with her male and female classmates. The school psychologist suggested that unless any concerns were voiced in the next several months, the team need not reconvene until the end of the school year. At that time, arrangements could be made for the following school year. •

Mike and Tabitha illustrate the types of school-aged children the school psychologist might assess. Mike's reading difficulties were compounded by a family problem. Tabitha's difficulties were much more complicated because of her age and disability. School psychologists administered tests in both cases, but they were only one part of the total assessment process.

Ethical Considerations for the School Psychologist Using Psychological Assessment

As with all of the applied psychologists described in previous chapters, school psychologists must be concerned about and dedicated to ethical procedures and practices. School psychologists should be especially diligent in adhering to these ethical issues because they tend to work exclusively with children and adolescents. Adults can quit their jobs if they do not like the tasks they have been assigned. Adults can choose to make an appointment with another psychologist or simply not schedule or show up for an appointment with a psychologist. Children either do not have the same options as adults or they may not be aware of their availability. A child who is having a problem in school may not know that such a person as a school psychologist even exists. Therefore, the psychologist in the schools has the following ethical responsibilities (beyond those of other psychologists):

1. He must always act in the best interests of the child.

2. She must make every effort to communicate to the child and to the parents or guardians of the child, in appropriate language, all rights and responsibilities involved in the assessment process.

3. He should communicate to all members of the school community (children, parents, and school personnel) the range of psychological services available and the means of obtaining these services.

4. She must be aware of new developments in the field that have an impact on practice.

5. He should treat all children fairly regardless of race, gender, family background, disability, or previous school experiences.

Concluding Remarks

As discussed in Chapter 2, the roles and functions of school psychologists are not limited to testing and assessment. Nonetheless, assessment-related duties, especially with disabled children, constitute a large part of most school psychologists' daily activities.

An alternative model exists for serving children with a variety of school-related difficulties. J. L. Graden, A. Casey, and S. L. Christenson (1985) proposed a **Prereferral Intervention System** as an indirect service model for the psychologist. Their system suggests and implements appropriate intervention strategies in the classroom before formal referral for psychological testing. Graden et al. state that the traditional model calls for a referral followed by psychological testing, usually leading to special education placement. Consequently, special education classes (which are extremely costly and may not always be the best long-term solution) are filled to overflowing.

In the Prereferral Intervention System, prior to a formal referral the school psychologist consults with the regular classroom teacher, and together they plan an appropriate intervention strategy for the specific problem behaviors. Only if all such strategies fail is a formal referral for testing initiated. The system suggested by Graden et al. has a number of benefits: it allows more children to stay in regular rather than special education classrooms; it provides regular education teachers with some new classroom strategies; and it frees school psychologists for more consultation with teachers and fewer time-consuming assessments. Whether such a system will be widely adopted and how it will work on a long-term basis remain to be seen.

ADDITIONAL READING

For more information about school psychology, consult the following sources.

Recent Books

Bergan, J. R. (Ed.). (1985). *School psychology in contemporary society: An introduction.* Columbus, OH: Charles E. Merrill.

Conoley, J. D., & Conoley, C. W. (1982). *School consultation: A guide to practice and training.* New York: Pergamon Press.

Curtis, M. J., & Zins, J. E. (Eds.). (1981). *The theory and practice of school consultation.* Springfield, IL: Charles C. Thomas.

Fairchild, T. N. (Ed.). (1977). *Accountability for school psychologists: Selected readings.* Washington, DC: University Press of America.

Hynd, G. W. (Ed.). (1983). *The school psychologist: An introduction.* Syracuse, NY: Syracuse University Press.

Kratochwill, T. R. (Ed.). (1981-1985). *Advances in school psychology* (Vols. 1-4). Hillsdale, NJ: Laurence Erlbaum Associates.

Maher, C. A., Illback, R. J., & Zins, J. E. (Eds.). (1984). *Organizational psychology in the schools: A handbook for professionals.* Springfield, IL: Charles C. Thomas.

Nolen, P. A. (1983). *School psychologist's handbook: Writing the educational report.* Springfield, IL: Charles C. Thomas.

Phye, G. D., & Reschly, D. J. (Eds.). (1979). *School psychology perspectives and issues.* New York: Academic Press.

Reynolds, C. R., Gutkin, T. B., Elliott, S. N., & Witt, J. C. (1984). *School psychology: Essentials of theory and practice.* New York: John Wiley and Sons.

Spadafore, G. J. (Ed.). (1981). *School psychology: Issues and answers.* Muncie, IN: Accelerated Development.

Thomas, A., & Grimes, J. (Eds.). (1985). Best practices in school psychology. Kent, OH: National Association of School Psychologists.

Ysseldyke, J. E. (Ed.). (1984). *School psychology: The state of the art.* Minneapolis, MN: University of Minnesota, National School Psychology Inservice Training Network.

Journals

Journal of School Psychology
School Psychology Review
Psychology in the Schools
Professional School Psychology

CHAPTER 7

Controversies

The first chapter of this book began with the statement that tests are neither helpful nor harmful in and of themselves. Rather, questions about and criticisms of psychological assessment procedures usually revolve around application of the test results to decisions directly affecting people's lives. Such applications go far beyond the concepts of reliability and validity and into legal and ethical questions that are perplexing, especially to those of us in the helping professions. This chapter will identify and address some of the major legal and ethical issues and controversies over the uses of psychological assessment in applied settings. The final section will discuss the relatively new but important controversy over the use of computers in the assessment process.

Psychological Assessment and the Law

According to a variety of sources (Anastasi, 1979; Brodsky, 1976; Fenster, et al., 1976), psychologists may be involved in nearly every aspect of the legal system. Clinical psychologists employed by police departments, for example, may screen prospective police officers, help in the training of police officers, and perform clinical services such as crisis intervention and even long-term therapy for officers and other department personnel. They may also be asked to provide staff-development opportunities on topics ranging from intervening in domestic squabbles to negotiating in a hostage situation. Frequently psychologists help the victims of crimes and counsel the families of police officers who have been injured or killed while on duty. Because of the nature of police work, a psychologist might be asked to conduct stress-reduction workshops or to deal with substance abusers. In addition, psychologists may serve as consultants in solving crimes. For example, a colleague of mine who has conducted research in the area of interpersonal attractiveness testified in a personal-injury suit. The plaintiff had sustained a severe facial injury, and my colleague was asked how much this damage to his attractiveness would "cost him" in his life. Psychologists may also play a role in custody or abuse cases—again providing expert testimony.

After the trial, psychologists continue to play important roles. Certainly a defendant who was declared not competent to stand trial or not guilty by reason of insanity would receive long-term psychotherapy, probably within an in-patient facility. The opinion of a psychologist may be necessary before such an individual is able to return to society.

Defendants who are sent to prison might also receive individual or group therapy as a part of their rehabilitation. In the best penal systems, inmates may undergo vocational assessments to link them to job-training programs in hopes of preventing recidivism when they are released.

The importance of psychological research within the legal system should not be ignored. Research efforts may help refine the police selection and training process, identify those personal and societal factors that increase the likelihood of criminal behavior, and assist in improving the rehabilitative qualities of the prison system.

The applications of psychological assessment data to the judicial system are almost limitless. For convenience, we can divide such applications into two broad categories:

- *Category 1: Legal cases resulting from the applications of psychological assessment.* Psychological assessment practices themselves are on trial.

- *Category 2: Legal cases introducing psychological assessment as evidence or support.* Psychological assessment results are used to "make" a case.

Category 1 contains cases that question the use of psychological tests as part of a decision-making process. In other words, the tests and testing practices are themselves "on trial." D. N. Bersoff (1981) suggests that such cases can be divided into three major parts or themes. Part 1 includes legal issues surrounding the relationship between educational tests and cultural bias. Part 2 includes legal issues surrounding the applications of employment testing to personnel decisions. Part 3 includes those cases concerning individuals' desires for increased public access to psychological testing. Summaries of each of these three subcategories follow. All three subcategories involve the applications of psychological assessment data to people's daily lives.

Psychological Testing in the Schools and Cultural Bias

The major question posed by legal challenges in this area is, Are traditional psychological tests in educational settings fair for all students regardless of race, ethnic background, and gender? A second, and more subtle, question is, What happens to children as a result of school testing? The legal challenges within this category focus primarily on intelligence testing conducted individually or in groups.

It should not be surprising that a universally acceptable definition of the construct *intelligence* has eluded us until now and will probably continue to do so. Every person, trained as a psychologist or not, has some notion of intelligent behavior, but few if any of those notions enjoy widespread popularity.

Much of what we have traditionally included in definitions of intelligence may in reality be the ability to function within a public school system that is geared toward middle-class, predominantly white children and adolescents. A child who experiences difficulty in such a school system may be given an individually administered "intelligence" test—a test that in all likelihood was developed by a white, middle-class psychologist who experienced success in that same public school system. Let us say that the child's performance on the test yields an IQ score of 68. Until fairly recently, that child would often almost automatically be placed in a special education class for the educable mentally retarded. Such a placement is often beneficial for educational and emotional reasons. Class size is kept to a minimum, and lessons are individualized to meet the needs of each child. (Indeed, it was my impression when I worked as a school psychologist that the special education teachers were often the best and most caring teachers in their schools.) Unfortunately, children in these classes may become labeled slow or retarded. Of course, such labels can be devastating emotionally to the child and the parents, as well as limiting the child's future educational and vocational prospects.

The first case specifically addressing the issue of the fairness of psychological testing within the public school system was *Hobson v. Hanson* (1967). In this case a disproportionate number of black children in Washington, D.C., were placed in lower-level classes based on results of group tests. The major issue raised by *Hobson v. Hanson* was whether the test results actually reflected the students' "innate abilities." The court found that the group tests used in this case were not sufficient to justify a student's placement in a low-ability level class. According to Bersoff (1982), *Hobson v. Hanson* "represents the condemnation of rigid, poorly conceived classification practices that negatively affect the educational opportunities of minority children" (p. 1047). In other words, the decision chastised the school district for engaging in practices resulting in limited educational options for minority-group children.

Two cases in the early 1970s (*Diana v. State of California*, 1970, and *Guadalupe v. Tempe Elementary District*, 1972) continued the process that *Hobson v. Hanson* started. The two cases were class-action suits brought on behalf of minority/bilingual students who had been placed in classes for the educable mentally retarded (EMR). Both suits concerned the misuses of traditional, primarily English tests of ability with students whose primary language was not English. The two cases were settled by agreement to modify psychological assessment practices and procedures consistent with the child's primary language.

The judgment in the *Guadalupe* case contained a requirement for the examination of **adaptive behavior** and other measures in addition to the use of intelligence tests for purposes of school classification. Adaptive behavior examines children's skills in getting along in their environment. Adaptive behavior scales often investigate a child's communication skills, self-help skills, abilities to run errands, make purchases, and so forth.

Certainly the most influential and publicized case along these lines has been *Larry P. v. Riles* (1972, 1974, 1979). The *Larry P.* case was a class-action suit filed on behalf of black children in the San Francisco school system. The major issue in *Larry P.* was similar to that of *Hobson v. Hanson*—the over-representation of minority students in EMR classes. Unlike *Hobson v. Hanson*, which blamed the use of group tests, *Larry P.* was based on the application of individual tests of intelligence. *Larry P. v. Riles* resulted in a ruling that prohibited the use of individual tests of intelligence with black children in California specifically for the purposes of special education class placement.

One additional case is worth noting. A case similar to *Larry P.* was tried in a federal district court in Illinois (*PASE v. Hannon*, 1980). The results of the so-called *PASE* case, however, were far different from the *Larry P.* decision. The judge in the *PASE* case concluded that few items on the most frequently administered individual IQ tests (WISC, WISC-R, and Stanford-Binet) were biased. The court also found that other sources of assessment data (not merely scores on tests) are essential in making decisions about educational classification and placement.

The Use of Employment Testing in Personnel Decisions

Psychological testing for purposes of job placement is another aspect of assessment that frequently finds its way into the courtroom. Accounts of such legal issues usually begin with a case known as *Griggs v. Duke Power Co.* In this case, black employees challenged the legality of general ability tests used by a private employer to hire and advance employees. The plaintiffs claimed that the use of such tests violated Title VII of the 1964 Civil Rights Act, which "prohibits discrimination in employment on the basis of race, religion, sex, or national origin" (Bersoff, 1981, p. 1050). The Duke Power Company was cited by the U.S. Supreme Court for using tests for purposes of hiring and promoting that were not necessarily related to the skills needed on the job. In other words, why should tests of general ability be used if a low score does not mean that the person cannot do the job?

In *Albemarle Paper Co. v. Moody* (1975), a company hired a psychologist to conduct a validation study of the general ability test it used. The psychologist compared test performances with supervisors' performance ratings of current employees. The U.S. Supreme Court criticized the validation study, saying it still did not determine what specific skills were needed on the job and whether the test could legitmately predict job performance.

Increased Access to Psychological Testing and Results of Testing

Two legal cases are of interest in this category. The first is the New York Truth in Testing Law, which primarily reflected a public interest group's investigation of the Educational Testing Service (ETS). According to R. M. Kaplan and D. P. Saccuzzo (1982), the New York Truth in Testing Law requires testing companies to "(1) disclose all studies on the validity of a test, (2) provide a complete disclosure to students about what scores mean and how they were calculated, and (3), on request by a student, provide a copy of the test questions, the correct answers, and the student's answers" (p. 473).

Part 3 is the most controversial portion of the law, for it means that anyone can request a copy of and answers to the Scholastic Aptitude Test (SAT), American College Testing (ACT), and so forth. In the past, test companies such as ETS used some of the same items on subsequent test forms. However, now that previous test forms are essentially open to public scrutiny, test companies must generate all original items for each new test form. The cost of this action has been large.

The other issue to be considered here concerns many of the issues addressed by Public Law 94-142 (parts of which were described in Chapter 6). Testing often acts as a "gatekeeper." That is, the results of testing may provide access to increased educational and occupational opportunities. To use an exaggerated metaphor, suppose the gatekeeper requires a password in English and the person trying to get through the gate speaks only Spanish or Vietnamese. Suppose the gatekeeper admits only white males who are not wheelchair-bound and so forth. Everyone should have the right to go through that gate, regardless of the necessary modifications. If a child speaks only Spanish, the psychologist must find someone who can administer tests in Spanish or at least locate an interpreter. Even if such a person can be located, translating the test verbatim from English to Spanish is not sufficient unless items and norms are relevant. Similarly a hearing-impaired job applicant has the right to be given every consideration. The testing must be reliable and must be valid for the educational program or job for which it is required.

As mentioned earlier, Category 1 is based on legal cases resulting from the applications of psychological assessment. Category 2 is composed of those cases in which psychological testing is used as evidence in a legal case. An example of Category 2 is the issue of criminal responsibility, or "not guilty by reason of insanity."

How do you decide if a person who committed a crime was "not guilty by reason of insanity"? Perhaps anyone who commits a violent crime can be considered "insane" in that such a crime in itself is not considered "sane" behavior. Alternatively, regardless of mental functioning, a person who committed a crime is clearly "guilty" of committing the criminal act. This particular issue has received a great deal of recent attention, primarily because of John Hinckley, the young man who attempted to assassinate Ronald Reagan. The Hinckley trial received a tremendous amount of publicity by virtue of the crime itself, but when Mr. Hinckley was declared "not guilty by reason of insanity," the publicity became almost a national outcry against the decision.

What role do psychologists and specifically psychological tests play in a decision such as this? Although their roles vary from case to case, psychologists and their assessment results may have a tremendous impact on such judgments. One or more psychologists might be asked to assess a defendant and then share the results of that assessment within the courtroom. In addition, a psychologist may be called as an **expert witness**. An expert witness not only presents factual data for the jury to consider but also gives an opinion about the matter at hand based on professional judgment and experience.

Psychologists might also be asked to provide testimony or to act as expert witnesses in cases involving issues other than the insanity plea. For example, consider the notion of **competence to stand trial**. A psychologist may believe, based on a variety of assessment procedures—interviews, observations, tests—that an individual is neither emotionally able to endure a trial nor sufficiently competent to participate in the proceedings.

At least two instruments have been developed specifically for the purpose of determining whether an individual is competent to stand trial. The Competency Screening Test (CST) is a sentence-completion procedure with questions about the individual's awareness of legal policies, procedures, and outcomes. The Competency to Stand Trial Assessment Instrument (CAI), developed by the same group of people who developed the CST, goes one step farther than the CST. The CAI contains items that are useful to the psychologist or psychiatrist in interviewing clients who were deemed not competent to stand trial as a result of the CST.

Another type of competence-related adjudication involves what might be called "competence to be self-sufficient." Is an individual sufficiently "fit" mentally or physically to take care of himself or herself as well as his or her financial and legal affairs? A psychological assessment in conjunction with a medical examination could prove invaluable to the people who must render the final decision in such cases.

Psychological assessment can be vital in liability and disability cases as well. Two roles come to mind for the psychologist conducting assessments in such cases. The first involves the introduction of assessment data as evidence of the individual's current functioning level. The psychologist would provide a description of the individual's performance during assessment, emphasizing areas of strength and weakness. In most cases, the psychologist would need to estimate the individual's level of function prior to the event (accident or illness) that led to the disability. For example, a psychologist might assume that a high school English teacher with a master's degree had an IQ of approximately 122 prior to an accident (the average IQ for teachers in a study of enlisted military personnel, Harrell & Harrell, 1945). If the teacher scores substantially below that level on postaccident testing, the psychologist may assume that the accident led to the decrease in cognitive functioning. On the other hand, a person working at a fairly menial job in a factory could have an IQ anywhere from below 70 to the upper extremes. Therefore, the psychologist might rely on interview data from family, co-workers, and so forth to estimate the person's level of functioning before the accident or illness.

If a psychologist has actually assessed a person prior to an accident or illness, that data could prove invaluable in determining the extent of damage. This provision of previous assessment data is the second function for psychologists in cases of disability/liability. Although psychological assessment instruments are far from perfect, they may be considerably more reliable than estimates of a person's previous intellectual abilities or personality characteristics based on reports of family and friends.

One final application of psychological assessment data within the legal system involves the use of psychological testimony in cases of child custody. With the current high divorce rate in the United States and elsewhere, it is hardly surprising that many psychologists and other mental health professionals spend a good deal of their time working with the "victims" of divorce—adults as well as children. Frequently, when the marriage has produced children, the dissolution of that marriage means deciding who should have child custody. A recent survey (Keilin & Bloom, 1986) examined the assessment practices of mental health professionals involved in child custody cases. Of the eighty-two respondents, more than three fourths were doctoral-level psychologists; the remainder were psychiatrists and master's-level practitioners.

In terms of actual assessment-related procedures conducted in their child custody cases, more than half of the professionals listed the following activities:

- Clinical interviews with mother and father individually.

- Clinical interviews with children (individually and together but without parents).

- Psychological testing of parents.

- Psychological testing of children.

- Observing mother-child and father-child interactions.

- Observing mother-father interactions.

At least half of all of the survey respondents reported these activities as vital to the evaluation process.

In terms of specific test instruments used in assessing parents and children for child custody cases, the MMPI was most frequently administered to parents. In fact, the MMPI was used by nearly twice as many professionals as the Rorschach, the second most frequently used instrument, or the Thematic Apperception Test (TAT), which ranked third. The Wechsler Adult Intelligence Scale (WAIS) was used by nearly 30 percent of the respondents. Many psychologists would question the wisdom of administering any or all of these tests to parents in child custody cases. What data do we have about the relationship between scores on any of these tests and a person's parenting skills?

For the "objects" of custody cases, the children, no single test was used by more than half of the respondents. Intelligence testing (for example, WISC, WAIS, Stanford-Binet) was used by 45 percent of respondents, whereas the TAT or CAT was used by 39 percent. Again, the reason for the administration of these tests is not completely clear.

In deciding who should receive custody of the children, the survey respondents try to give primary consideration to the wishes of the child, especially when older children (aged ten and up) are involved. Other factors taken into consideration are the relationship between each parent and the child(ren), the psychological stability of the parents, the relationship between the parents, and the laws of the state in which the case is tried.

In this section I have attempted to condense a tremendously wide and growing area into a few pages. Readers interested in learning more about the legal aspects of psychological assessment will find additional references at the conclusion of this chapter.

Ethical Controversies

Let us begin our discussion of the ethics of psychological assessment in applied settings with two extreme examples. First, suppose that the following article appears on the front page of your daily newspaper.

Testing Determines Youth Employment Opportunities

Based on the results of a new city-wide testing program, Normtown's high school students have been told what jobs they may obtain on graduation. Twenty percent of the students will be permitted to go to college in preselected fields, 25 percent will receive vocational training, 30 percent will be employed by the city in specific jobs for which they qualified, and 15 percent will be employed by private businesses. The remaining 10 percent were deemed unemployable on the basis of their test scores. Their names will be placed on the welfare rolls, and they will be ineligible to work.

The coordinator of the testing program believes that this program has several advantages: "First, it will eliminate the need for young people to make these difficult decisions for themselves. Second, we will be able to meet all of the city's employment needs. Third, it will get the right person in the right job."

When asked about the apparent imbalance in certain categories along racial and economic lines, the testing coordinator responded, "That's the way the test results came out. It's not our fault."

Normtown's mayor was not available for comment. A report from a close adviser of the mayor, however, indicates that the mayor is in seclusion after learning that her daughter's scores qualify her for the welfare category.

What is wrong with this scenario? Was the test good or bad? Was it valid? Was it reliable?

At this point, we know nothing about the test. It may have been highly valid and reliable. Our quarrel is not with the test. It is with the application of the test results. The context in which the test was interpreted is such that our basic sensibilities are threatened. No weight was given to freedom of choice, not to mention such characteristics as an individual's motivation, interpersonal abilities, or interests. Test scores alone were the basis for vocational decisions.

Now for the second example.

Assessing the Candidates: A Scientific Approach to Electing a President

A recent poll indicated that most Americans are not interested in candidates' opinions on nuclear arms, civil rights, or the national debt. Instead, those polled claimed that they want to know what each candidate is "really like." One citizen summed up his thoughts on the issue as follows: "Most of the candidates do not have enough of the necessary background information to know what decisions they will actually make on the job. I want to know that our next president has a strong mix of intelligence, compassion, and leadership to make the right choices when all of the facts are in."

In order to meet this desire for personal information about the candidates, several of the country's top-rated psychologists will be asked to meet with the candidates individually and administer to them a battery of psychological tests and other assessment techniques. Results will then be made available to the media to pass along to the public. The tests and other techniques to be used include the following:

Wechsler Adult Intelligence Scale—Revised
Minnesota Multiphasic Personality Inventory
Strong-Campbell Interest Inventory
Rorschach
Study of Values
Peabody Individual Achievement Test

The results of these tests, along with information from personal interviews and behavioral observations, will be integrated into a psychological report-type format for each candidate.

What is wrong with this example? Certainly, very few people in this country believe that in every presidential election the "best person for the job" has triumphed. The problem is that psychological assessment may not be any better and may, in fact, be worse at picking a president than a majority of voters. We have no data about the predictive validity of psychological tests in cases of presidential elections. What do we expect to gain from such test data? If one person has an IQ score on the WAIS-R of 145 and another has a score of 125, will the first be a better president? And what do we mean by a "better president"? We also have the question of influence. Is there any reason that psychological tests or psychologists themselves, for that matter, should possess the clout to influence the election of world leaders? Finally—and this is not an issue to be taken lightly—do candidates for public office have a right to protect their own privacy?

Although both of these examples may seem extreme, at least under our democratic form of government, many decisions based primarily on the results of test performance do affect the lives of people of all ages. While writing this book, I had many discussions about its content with friends and acquaintances—some of whom are psychologists and others of whom are not. Nearly every discussion included examples of how tests had affected people's lives. One couple had been told that their five-year-old son scored in the "borderline-retarded" category based on an IQ test. That "retarded" boy now has a master's degree and is a successful professional. Other people (some of whom now have PhDs) were counseled in high school that they would never succeed in a college atmosphere based on their college aptitude tests. Still others with seemingly unlimited potential based on test results have not been particularly successful, at least in any traditional way (educationally, professionally, or financially).

One elderly woman, on finding out that I was a psychologist who administered tests, said that she recalled taking an IQ test when she was in fourth grade. She had always been bothered by the answer to one particular question in the test. She described the question, and I recognized it as one on the Stanford-Binet. She remarked that she had answered the question a certain way and then looked up at the examiner for a sign of approval. The examiner had not provided such a cue (examiners are not supposed to provide any positive or negative feedback during testing), so she had changed her answer in the hopes of getting a more positive response from him. After all of these years (at least fifty), she was still seeking reassurance that her original answer was correct. It was correct, and I told her so and explained that examiners are supposed to remain neutral rather than give any cues about the test taker's performance. Imagine how disturbing this experience must have been for this woman to recall the question and her response fifty years later.

Psychologists and psychological tests carry a lot of influence in our society. As I mentioned earlier in this book, through the use of psychological assessment data, psychologists often act as gatekeepers in making important decisions: Who should be placed in special education classes? Who should be hired and promoted? Who should be found not guilty by reason of insanity? Psychologists usually make these decisions in consultation with others. Nonetheless, the psychologist is often considered the expert, and the assessment data are often treated as facts. If our assessment techniques were 100 percent accurate, this gatekeeping role might be less controversial. Because psychological tests and other assessment techniques are far from perfect, caution must be exercised in using assessment information in such critical decisions.

The Mystique of Psychological Assessment

There is nothing magical about assessment in general or testing in particular. This fact is disappointing to some consumers of psychological tests and reassuring to others. The perception remains in many people, however, that through testing and assessment procedures the "real person" will be magically revealed, stripped of defense mechanisms and other deceptions.

The assessment procedures available today, when used by an experienced, astute professional, should offer information about a client's general functioning level, along with information about strengths and weaknesses, approaches to problem solving, level of self-esteem, interpersonal interaction style, and so forth. Frequently, clients themselves and their parents, teachers, employers, and friends already know this information.

In my own work, I find it helpful to preface my presentation of assessment data to clients with a statement such as "Many, if not most, of my findings should sound familiar to you." Then, when I mention particular areas of strength or weakness, I try to provide a lot of examples from the natural environment. For example, if an individual seemed fairly rigid in his approach to tasks, I will say to him, "You seemed to get pretty frustrated when your first try didn't work out" or I will say to his parents, "I'll bet he gives up easily when a problem comes up."

Many individuals seem to view the assessment process itself as a partial, if not total, cure for their problems. Needless to say, these individuals are almost invariably disappointed. The word *almost* in the previous sentence is intentional. I have had the rare experience of interpreting test results to a person and seeing that person's outlook on life change immediately. I recall a six-year-old boy who had been referred to me by his teachers because he was having difficulty in school. In the course of administering the Wechsler Intelligence Scale for Children—Revised, I discovered that this little boy could define any word in dictionary-precise terms, explain the differences and similarities between any two terms, and solve some fairly difficult arithmetic problems in his head. On the other hand, his skills at block design and object assembly were dreadful. After we were finished, I made some statement about strengths and weaknesses such as "You know you're a very smart young man, but I see that you do have trouble doing certain kinds of things. Let's see if we can get you some kind of help with your difficulties while you keep on building on those strengths." This little boy smiled so broadly and said "You mean I'm not really dumb? There are just some things I can't do as well as other kids?" I said, "Yes, but there are a lot of things you do better than most other kids." He proceeded to list the things he could and could not do well—a list more accurate and insightful than most adults could provide about themselves. He seemed reassured that someone else understood him and that his self-perceptions were substantiated.

Notice, however, that the results of the assessment process described here were neither magical nor surprising. Instead, the testing provided me with an opportunity to find out in a couple of hours some of the things that a six-year-old boy had discovered about himself over time.

Sometimes the results of testing can have unpleasant ramifications for people. In the undergraduate psychological tests and measurements class that I teach, students are subjected to a number of psychological tests throughout the semester-long course. The tests are administered to illustrate the process of assessment. I want students to know first-hand what it feels like to take these tests and to interpret them. I hope that through the experience, students will develop what I call a "healthy skepticism" about psychological assessment procedures.

The first test that I have students take is the Goodenough Draw-A-Man Test. I simply ask students to draw a picture of a man. We then score their drawings for an approximate developmental level. After completing these procedures, I ask the students, "What do you think of this as a measure of development? Is it a fairly accurate assessment of how you see yourself?" Usually students are amused and slightly embarrassed by having to draw any sort of picture in a college classroom, and a lively discussion ensues.

Several years ago, a woman in the class followed me to my office after that class. She was an older student (about forty) whom I had seen around the psychology department on other occasions. She always seemed nervous or unsure of herself, even though she was a graduating senior who had already been accepted to several master's-level graduate programs. Upon arriving at my office she said, "This drawing test is right!" I asked her to explain what she meant, and she said that her score of 70 on the test confirmed what she had always thought her true IQ score to be. She said that on the other tests she had taken she came out as bright-normal or better, but she always knew that they were wrong. Now she had proof—her developmental score on the Draw-A-Man confirmed her worst suspicions. Oddly enough, she seemed relieved that this information was now out in the open.

We talked for a long time about her feelings. Gradually, she became convinced that many people feel like "imposters" waiting to be found out. I tried to emphasize that the Goodenough Draw-A-Man test is rarely used with adults to assess ability and aptitude and that her previous tests were much more valid as measures of her actual academic success.

This incident increased my awareness of the importance some individuals place on a particular psychological testing experience. Such experiences have helped me to see the mystique that psychologists and psychological tests have for certain people and have made me increasingly cautious in my own uses of assessment procedures. Testing is a tool for psychologists, but it can be an extremely powerful tool, and caution must be exercised in order for testing to be used properly.

The Computer Controversy

It would be difficult to find a more controversial topic in the current assessment literature than the use of computers in the assessment process. Opinions on computerized assessment range from those who view computers as a divine gift to psychologists to those who view computers as a foolish fad (at best) and a terrible curse at worst. Most of us sit somewhat awkwardly in the middle on this issue, waiting to be convinced one way or the other.

Let us begin our discussion of this controversial topic with an examination of some of the advantages and disadvantages involved in using computers at each step of the assessment process.

Referral Information

The information contained on most referral forms includes identifying data (name, address, date of birth, gender) and some type of referral question or reason for the referral request. The advantages of putting such information directly into the computer are many. First, there are the pragmatic advantages—no papers, pens, paper clips, piles of reports, or file folders to drag around, less danger of loss, no problems deciphering handwriting, and so forth. (If you think these advantages are trivial, you have never worked in an office.) The computerized referral system can also facilitate research projects. In the past, if I wanted to study gender differences in "reason for referral to school psychologists" among second graders in public schools, I would have to spend considerable time searching through a lot of file cabinets trying to locate material. Imagine, however, a computer program available to do all of the searching for me and provide me with gender-specific lists of reasons for referral. The prospect is wonderful and undoubtedly already available in some school systems. After all, it is not so different from the on-line computer searches available on any topic in many libraries.

The major disadvantages of using computers to collect referral data concern confidentiality. Does the use of a computer have an impact on a client's right to confidentiality? My answer would have to be probably not. The danger that an unauthorized person will gain access to such information is probably no greater than the danger of someone reading a file folder or overhearing a private conversation. On the other hand, clients might get a "false sense of confidentiality" with a computer, forgetting that others can gain access to the information. Another possible disadvantage of using a computer for referral data may be that the computer itself becomes more important than the client's feelings and responses.

Interview Data

There are several ways of integrating computer technology into the assessment interview. First, the client can be interviewed by the computer itself. In such cases, the computer prints a question and the person types a response. Some authors have discovered that people may actually be more candid in answering sensitive questions (for example, those regarding sexual problems or substance abuse problems) posed by a computer than those posed by a person. Computers do not notice blushes, tears, or trembling during an interview. Of course, computers must be programmed to ask a client to "tell me more about that." A disadvantage is that many people, particularly elderly people, may be extremely intimidated at the thought of using a computer.

When computers are used by an interviewer to record responses, pragmatic matters such as fatigue and illegible handwriting may improve. On the other hand, imagine the impact on client-psychologist rapport when the computer (or computer operator) malfunctions in the middle of an interview.

Previous Records and Reports

The use of a computer to "call up" previous records about a client may be an extremely efficient means of accessing that information, assuming, of course, that such records have been saved and are on a disk that is compatible with present technological systems. Aside from things that can go wrong, one drawback may be that by switching records to an automated format, only the basic data about a person will be included—name, age, dates of referral, reason for referral, scores on tests, and so forth. The actual test responses, the child's drawings, the teenager's homework, or the office manager's memos will be gone. As with several other steps, automation may depersonalize previous records and reports.

Observational Data

This is the stage of assessment that may suffer most as testing becomes increasingly computerized. Individual administration of psychological testing provides the psychologist with an excellent opportunity to observe a client "in action." How does a man respond to questions? Does he call out the first thing that comes to mind, or does he sit back and ponder the question and response? How does a woman deal with praise? Does she brighten when complimented or does she look away and mumble, "It was no big deal, anyone could do it"? Can the boy described by his teacher as hyperactive sit still for half an hour or is he in constant motion? Is this twelve-year-old girl as shy as her parents think she is? Even if the psychologist were to observe the client interacting with the computer, the observations would not allow for the same kind of interpersonal data provided in the one-to-one testing situation.

Testing

How does taking a computerized test affect test performance? Here, too, there are strengths and drawbacks. A client can take a test at his or her own convenience rather than at the convenience of a psychologist. Computers can be programmed to allow for response-contingent testing. That is, if a client misses a question, the computer returns to an easier question; if a client gets two answers correct, the computer advances to more difficult questions. In such cases, clients may answer fewer questions overall than they would if they were taking a test themselves or having an examiner administer a test.

Some clients may find computerized testing far more interesting than paper and pencil testing, thus increasing motivation and diligence. Also, as mentioned earlier in this chapter, clients may be more candid when answering questions on personality inventories about sensitive issues such as sexual problems.

Computers can also be programmed to present items at regular time intervals and to note the "lag time" between the presentation of a question and the client's response. When a longer than usual amount of time elapses, it might signal the psychologist that a sensitive area exists.

Computerized testing has disadvantages as well. Clients who are unfamiliar with computers may be uncomfortable or anxious about the testing process. These reactions may adversely affect test performances. (Training sessions have been found to help.)

In addition, most children up to about age eight and many older individuals lack the reading proficiency necessary for most automated testing. For school psychologists who test a large number of children and adolescents referred for reading difficulties, this is a major drawback.

Computer testing may also give an individual a false sense of confidentiality or anonymity. The client may forget or not realize that a person will be reviewing responses to test items.

Because computers save time and effort, psychologists may favor those tests that have been computerized even though a noncomputerized test might be more appropriate. Agencies and institutions could conceivably put pressure on psychologists to streamline their assessments by using computerized assessment instruments as much as possible.

Scoring, Interpreting, and Reporting Test Results

The use of computers to score, interpret, and report test results is more widespread than in other areas and is probably more controversial for that reason. If computer programs were limited to the scoring of objective tests, psychologists would either be delighted or at least would not protest too vehemently. The hand-scoring process tends to be quite tedious, and anything that speeds up that process would no doubt be welcomed with open arms (at least to those professionals who have access to a computer and who can convince the business office to purchase the appropriate software).

What about scoring less objective tests? Can the computer decide when to give credit on an ambiguous response? Computer scoring loses some popularity in such cases. What makes the software developer better at scoring than a psychologist? It becomes a matter of one professional's word against another's.

How about projective tests? Can a computer program reliably respond to stimuli developed for their ambiguity? These are questions that have not yet been answered.

The debates become even more intense when the issue is test interpretation. Perhaps the strongest argument is merely a variation on an old theme— **clinical judgment versus the actuarial approach**. This question has been argued for years—at least since P. E. Meehl's Midwestern Psychological Association presidential address (1955). This question challenges the basic tenets of applied psychology in asking whether we might be better off removing as much of the psychologist's subjective judgment as possible from the assessment process. Proponents argue that the more objective the processes of test administration, scoring, and interpretation, the more useful the results will be and the more seriously psychological testing will be taken. Opponents of this "actuarial approach" to assessment argue just as vehemently that such an approach is tantamount to removing the heart and soul of psychology. Is there no value in considering the behavioral observations of an experienced examiner? Can a computerized assessment system match the insights of a trained psychologist?

A second issue concerning the computer interpretation of tests involves the phenomenon often called "garbage in-garbage out." That is, if the computer is fed inaccurate or meaningless information, then the output will not be accurate either. Are the computer interpretations better than or at least equal to the interpretations provided by psychologists in terms of validity, reliability, sensitivity to demographic variables, and other critical characteristics? Again, this is not an easily answered question. It is certainly true that computer interpretations may be deficient in validity and reliability, but the same can be true for interpretations by two different psychologists or by one psychologist on two or more occasions.

The critical question may not be "Are computer-generated interpretations as good as clinical interpretations?" but rather "Do psychologists and their clients unjustifiably put more trust into the impressive computer interpretative systems, thus believing them to be more scientific and more accurate than interpretations by mere mortals?" Most of us have compared handwritten reports with type-written copies of the same reports. Surely the typewritten copy appears more authoritative and more credible. Imagine the effect of seeing a report interpreted and printed by a computer. Some interpretive systems even contain graphic displays of data.

The psychologist who cushions interpretive statements with phrases such as "it seems to me . . ." or "I believe that you . . ." is going to be overpowered by scientific-looking and definitive-sounding interpretations even though her statements are probably more appropriate given the state of the art and science of psychological test interpretation.

Accessibility to software presents another problem with computerized test scoring and interpretation. Should anyone be able to buy such software or should distribution be restricted to psychologists? How about physicians? Psychiatrists? Educators? Counselors?

Overall, computers represent a mixed blessing to the field of psychological assessment. From one perspective, the concept is exciting, and the possible applications seem limitless. The benefits in savings of time and money are abundant. From the opposite perspective, psychologists must weigh the benefits against the drawbacks of depersonalization, overacceptance of imperfect software, the possible loss of rich observational and anecdotal data, and the tendency to view computerized reports as more authoritative than the reports of an individual psychologist.

The developers, distributers, and users of automated assessment procedures must temper their enthusiasm with skepticism. They must not forget that each person who undergoes psychological assessment procedures is an individual whose life may be affected by the results. These few pages have provided an overview of some of the issues involved in using computers in the psychological assessment process. Additional references are listed at the conclusion of this chapter.

Concluding Remarks

Because of the mystique of psychological testing, those of us who recommend, administer, and interpret such tests have a strong ethical responsibility to our professions and to the public. We must be aware of professional and societal developments that have an impact on testing. At the same time, we must be skeptical of new methods and techniques; we should never embrace a new development wholeheartedly before thoroughly weighing its advantages and disadvantages.

ADDITIONAL READING

For more information about the application of psychological assessment techniques to the legal system, consult the following sources:

Bersoff, D. N. (1982). The legal regulation of school psychology. In Reynolds, C. R., & Gutkin, T. B. (Eds.). *The handbook of school psychology.* New York: John Wiley and Sons.

Bersoff, D. N. (1981). Testing and the law. *American Psychologist, 36,* 1047–1056.

Farrington, P., Hawkins, K., & Lloyd-Bostock, S. M. (Eds.). (1979). *Psychology, law and legal processes.* Atlantic Highland, NJ: Humanities Press.

Fersch, E. A. (1979). Rethinking treatment of the young and disturbed. *Law, psychology, and the courts.* Springfield, IL: Charles C. Thomas.

Fields, F. R. J., & Horwitz, R. J. (Eds.). (1982). *Psychology and professional practice: The interface of psychology and the law.* Westport, CT: Quorum Books.

Keilin, W. G., & Bloom, L. J. (1986). Child custody evaluation practices: A survey of experienced professionals. *Professional Psychology: Research and Practice, 17,* 338–346.

Lanyon, R. I. (1986). Psychological assessment procedures in court-related settings. *Professional Psychology: Research and Practice, 17,* 260–268.

Melton, G. B., Petrila, J., Poythress, N. G., & Slobogin, C. (1987). *Psychological evaluations for the courts: A handbook for mental health professionals and lawyers.* New York: Guilford Press.

Muller, D. J., Blackman, D. E., & Chapman, A. J. (Eds.). (1984). *Psychology and law.* Chichester, England: John Wiley and Sons.

Rosen, R. H. (1983). The need for training in forensic child psychology. *Professional Psychology: Research and Practice, 14,* 481–489.

Sales, B. D. (Ed.). (1977). *Psychology in the legal process.* New York: Spectrum Publications, Inc.

Schwitzgebel, R. L., & Schwitzgebel, R. K. (1980). *Law and psychological practice.* New York: John Wiley and Sons.

Tapp, J. L., & Levine, F. J. (1977). *Law, justice, and the individual in society: Psychological and legal issues.* New York: Holt, Rinehart & Winston.

For more information about ethical issues relevant to psychological assessment, see the following sources:

American Psychological Association. (1977). *Ethical standards for psychological research.* Washington, DC: American Psychological Association.

American Psychological Association. (1981). Ethical principles of psychologists. *American Psychologist, 36,* 633–638.

Berndt, D. J. (1983). Ethical and professional considerations in psychological assessment. *Professional Psychology: Research and Practice, 14,* 580–587.

Haas, L. J., & Fennimore, D. (1983). Ethical and legal issues in professional psychology: Selected works, 1970–1981. *Professional Psychological Research and Practice, 14,* 540–548.

National Association of School Psychologists. (1985, January). *Professional conduct manual.* Washington, DC: National Association of School Psychologists. (Includes 1984 principles for professional ethics, and revised standards for the provision of psychological services.)

Schwitzgebel, R. K. (1978). Suggestions for uses of psychological devices in accord with legal and ethical standards. *Professional Psychology, 9,* 478–488.

Standards for educational and psychological testing (1985). Washington, DC: American Psychological Association.

For more information about the applications of computer technology to psychological assessment techniques, see:

Altemose, J. R., & Williamson, K. B. (1981). Clinical judgment vs. the computer: Can the school psychologist be replaced by a machine? *Psychology in the Schools, 18,* 356–363.

Bersoff, D. N. (1983). *A rationale and proposal regarding standards for the administration and interpretation of computerized psychological testing.* Baltimore, MD: Report prepared for Psychology Systems.

Brown, D. T. (1984). Automated assessment systems in school and clinical psychology: Present status—future directions. *School Psychology Review, 13,* 455–460.

Burke, M. J., & Normand, J. (1987). Computerized psychological testing: Overview and critique. *Professional Psychology: Research and Practice, 18,* 42–51.

Colorado Psychological Association. (1982). *Guidelines for the use of computerized testing services.* Denver: Colorado Pyschological Association.

Denner, S. (1977). Automated psychological testing: A review. *British Journal of Social and Clinical Psychology, 16,* 173–179.

Hafer, P. J., & Bersoff, D. N. (1984). *Standards for the administration and interpretation of computerized psychological testing.* Unpublished manuscript (available from D. N. Bersoff, Suite 511, 1200 Seventeenth St., N.W., Washington, DC 20036).

Skinner, H. A., & Pakula, A. (1986). Challenge of computers in psychological assessment. *Professional psychology: Research and Practice, 17,* 44–50.

CHAPTER 8

Final Comments

In this book we have looked at a wide range of issues relevant to the current uses of psychological assessment tools and techniques by psychologists working in applied settings. A book on the same topic written ten years ago would have been markedly different in content as well as emphasis. The notion of a person taking a psychological test given by a computer (see Chapter 7) was, if not unheard of, then at best, a remote possibility for most psychologists. The ramifications of such legislation as Public Law 94-142 (see Chapter 6) were just beginning to be realized in the late 1970s. Legal decisions such as *Larry P. v. Riles* and the *PASE* case (see Chapter 7) were just being heard. The world has changed a great deal in the past ten years, and psychological testing has changed with it.

I have frequently emphasized the impact that decisions based on the results of psychological assessment techniques can have on people's lives. Psychologists using such techniques to make important decisions have a formidable responsibility to adhere to the highest professional and ethical standards. A routine battery of tests for every client regardless of age, race, gender, cultural background, primary language, and disability clearly does not meet these standards.

In addition to the impact of psychological assessment on people's lives, psychological assessment has also been influenced by and has reflected many societal trends and changes. Both the women's movement and the civil rights movement have had a major impact on the development and modification of many of the test instruments and on the manner in which the tests are administered and the test data are used. Over the years there has been an increased sensitivity to the differences between cultures, between socioeconomic classes, between males and females, and between individuals at different stages of life. There has also been a greater emphasis on the whole continuum of disabilities.

Changes within the medical profession have had an impact on the clinical psychologist's assessment practices. The increased interest in brain-behavior relationships from both medical and psychological perspectives has caused neuropsychological assessment (as described in Chapter 3) to blossom in the past decade. Neuropsychology has been particularly influential in school psychology, notably in the assessment and treatment of children with learning disabilities.

Changes within a variety of disciplines as well as societal changes have greatly modified the assessment practices of counseling psychologists. For example, counseling psychologists employed by university counseling centers have had to deal with assessment and placement decisions regarding "nontraditional" students. Such a label often refers to older students who are returning to the college environment following many years of "life experiences," such as raising a family. Frequently, these students call on counseling psychologists to help evaluate their life experiences (that is, can any of the skills they have accumulated over the years count toward college credits?). The practice of counseling psychology has also reflected societal changes in substance-abuse patterns and the need for increased attention to crisis-intervention skills.

Recent changes in businesses and industries, judicial decisions, and the women's and civil rights movements have had an enormous combined impact on personnel testing for the industrial/organizational psychologist. As discussed in Chapter 5, the psychological testing portions of personnel assessment widely used a decade or so ago are no longer acceptable, and new practices, such as the assessment center concept, have been instituted.

Changes in education have had an overall impact on the practice of school psychology and on assessment practices of school psychologists in particular. Two fairly recent emphases in school psychology assessment practices are early childhood assessment for youngsters from birth to six years of age and vocational assessment, particularly for high-school-aged disabled youngsters. Both of these emphases reflect educational research coupled with legislative and political decisions. The responsibility of the public schools no longer starts automatically at age five and ends at age eighteen. As a result, the role of the school psychologist has expanded.

Psychological assessment procedures have an impact on many facets of our lives, but many factors also have an effect on psychological assessment procedures. Keeping up with the trends and issues in psychological assessment practices over the past decade has been an exciting, challenging, and often frustrating full-time job for many concerned professionals.

Because the field of psychological assessment has changed so rapidly within the past years, it is nearly impossible to predict what the next ten years will bring. Will there be a return to more traditional assessment practices emphasizing the use of IQ or ability tests, or will there be an increasing trend to prohibit the use of data from such tests for purposes of classification or placement of individuals in schools or businesses?

Is it possible to envision a world without any form of psychological assessment? Could such a world exist? Is such an existence an improvement over what we have now? Assessment as defined in this book is so broad a concept—

encompassing everything from observations to interviews to standardized tests—that it will probably always be with us in some form. The precise forms and directions that psychological assessment may take in the future, however, lead to some interesting speculations.

A personnel director of a large corporation hires a computer operator. He cannot use any assessment techniques—no observations, interviews, reports from others, and above all, no psychological tests. What is left? Little more than a random selection process somewhat akin to picking a name from a hat. It is true that a random selection procedure gives each job candidate an equal chance and that variables such as age, race, gender, and marital status are not used to discriminate against any candidates. On the other hand, the person selected may not possess the necessary skills for the job or may have been fired from his last ten positions for stealing from the company or starting fights with co-workers. In other words, our "fair" and unbiased system is not fair to the company, who did not necessarily get the best person for the job, nor was it fair to the qualified applicants for the job, who were not given any sort of special consideration for their training and skills.

Similar scenarios can be devised for school systems, counseling centers, and clinics. Psychological tests are designed to meet certain needs within societies. Taking away the tests does not remove the need. Children will continue to learn at their own speed with or without achievement tests to measure their progress. Adolescents will continue to struggle with issues such as "Who am I and where am I going?" with or without vocational interest tests, college entrance examinations, and self-esteem scales. Adults will continue to seek employment with or without interviews, letters of recommendation, and vocational aptitude tests.

Psychological assessment procedures can assist in many of these decisions and processes. These procedures are imperfect—no one stands behind any test or other psychological assessment procedure 100 percent. All that we can say is that in many cases, decisions based on the psychological assessment data are probably a little fairer and a little more informed than decisions based on other sources.

I would like to think that assessment techniques will be continually modified, refined, and employed in a rational manner when psychologists make important decisions. I hope that consumers of psychological tests will continue to be alert to inappropriate or unethical applications of these techniques. Finally, I hope that many of you who wish to pursue your studies in psychology will remember the importance of carefully planned, executed, and interpreted research studies, especially in applied psychological assessment—an area that has an impact on so many lives.

APPENDIX

Psychological Tests

Below is a list of all psychological tests mentioned in this book. Names of publishers are also provided for each test in the list. Readers wishing additional information about any psychological test should consult one or more of the following reference books:

Goldman, B. A., & Busch, J. C. (1982). *Directory of unpublished experimental measures* (Vol. 1–3). New York: Human Sciences Press.

Johnson, O. G. (1976). *Tests and measurements in child development: Handbook II* (Vol. 1 & 2). San Francisco: Jossey– Bass.

Keyser, D. J., & Sweetland, R. C. (Eds.). (1985). *Test critiques* (Vols. 1–5). Kansas City, MO: Test Corporation of America.

Mitchell, J. V. (Ed.). (1983). Tests in print III. Lincoln, NE: Buros Institute of Mental Measurements.

Mitchell, J. V. (Ed.). (1985). *The ninth mental measurements yearbook.* Lincoln, NE: Buros Institute of Mental Measurements.

Sweetland, R. C., & Keyser, D. J. (Eds.). (1983). *Tests: A comprehensive reference for assessments in psychology, education, and business.* Kansas City, MO: Test Corporation of America.

Test/Publisher

AAMD Adaptive Behavior Scale Public School Version—Revised
CTB/McGraw–Hill

ACT
American College Testing Program

Bender–Gestalt Visual Motor Test
American Orthopsychiatric Assn., Inc.

Biographical Information Blank (BIB)
Source: W. A. Owens, "Biographical data," in Dunnette, 1976.

Children's Apperception Test (CAT)
C.P.S., Inc.

College Board Scholastic Aptitude Test (SAT)
Educational Testing Service (ETS)

Columbia Mental Maturity Scale (CMMS)
Psychological Corporation

Competency Screening Test (CST)
Competency to Stand Trial Assessment Instrument (CAI)
Source: *American Journal of Psychiatry* (1971), *128*, 105.

Edwards Personal Preference Schedule
Psychological Corporation

Goodenough–Harris Drawing Test
Psychological Corporation

Graduate Record Examination (GRE)
Educational Testing Service

Halstead–Reitan Neuropsychological Battery
Halstead Neuropsychological Laboratories

House–Tree–Person Techniques: Revise Manual (H-T-P)
Western Psychological Services

Kuder Occupational Interest Survey, Form DD
Science Research Associates, Inc.

Luria–Nebraska Neuropsychological Battery
Western Psychological Services

Marital Satisfaction Index (MSI)
Western Psychological Services

Minnesota Multiphasic Personality Inventory (MMPI)
University of Minnesota Press

Mooney Problem Checklist
Psychological Corporation

Nelson–Denny Reading Test
Riverside Publishing Company

Peabody Individual Achievement Test (PIAT)
American Guidance Services

Peabody Picture Vocabulary Test—Revised (PPVT-R)
American Guidance Services

Personality Inventory for Children (PIC)
Western Psychological Services

Position Analysis Questionnaire (PAQ)
Purdue Research Foundation
University Book Store

Rorschach Psychodiagnoistic Test
Huber, Hans; distributed by Grune & Stratton, U.S.A.

Rotter Incomplete Sentences Blank
Psychological Corporation

Self Directed Search (SDS)
Psychological Assessment Resources (PAR)

Sixteen Personality Factors (16PF)
Institute for Personality & Ability Testing (IPAT)

Stanford–Binet Intelligence Scale, Fourth Edition
Riverside Publishing Company

Strong–Campbell Interest Inventory (SCII)
Stanford University Press

Study of Values
Riverside Publishing Company

Survey of Study Habits and Attitudes
Psychological Corporation

Thematic Apperception Test (TAT)
Harvard University Press

Wechsler Adult Intelligence Scale (WAIS)
Wechsler Adult Intelligence Scale—Revised (WAIS-R)
Psychological Corporation

Wechsler Intelligence Scale for Children (WISC)
Wechsler Intelligence Scale for Children—Revised (WISC-R)
Psychological Corporation

Woodcock–Johnson Psychoeducational Battery (WJPEB)
DLM Teaching Resources

References

Albright, L. E. et al. (1976). Federal government in psychological testing: Is it here? A symposium. *Personnel Psychology, 29,* 519–557.

American Psychiatric Association. (1980). *Diagnostic and statistical manual of mental disorders* (3rd ed.). Washington, DC: American Psychiatric Association.

American Psychological Association. (1984). *Graduate study in psychology and associated fields.* Washington, DC: American Psychological Association.

American Psychological Association. (1970). *A career in psychology.* Washington, DC: American Psychological Association.

Anastasi, A. (1979). *Fields of applied psychology* (2nd ed.). New York: McGraw-Hill.

Anastasi, A. (1981). Coaching, test sophistication, and developed abilities. *American Psychologist, 36,* 1086–1093.

Annis, L. V., Tucker, G. H., & Baker, C. A. (1984). APA certification of terminal master's degree programs. *American Psychologist, 39,* 563–566.

Asher, J., & Asher, J. (1978). Setting psychology's house in order. *APA Monitor, 8,* 44.

Batsche, G. M., & Peterson, D. W. (1983). School psychology and projective assessment: A growing incompatibility. *School Psychology Review, 12,* 440–445.

Bersoff, D. N. (1973). Silk purses into sows' ears: The decline of psychological testing and a suggestion for its redemption. *American Psychologist, 28,* 892–899.

Bersoff, D. N. (1981). Testing and the law. *American Psychologist, 36,* 1047–1056.

Bersoff, D. (1982). The legal regulation of school psychology. In C. R. Reynolds & T. B. Gutkin (Eds.), *The handbook of school psychology.* New York: John Wiley and Sons.

Bowers, N. E. (1971). Public reaction and psychological testing in the schools. *Journal of School Psychology, 9,* 114–119.

Breger, L. (1968). Psychological testing: Treatment and research implications. *Journal of Consulting and Clinical Psychology, 32,* 176–181.

Brodsky, S. L. (1976). Psychology and criminal justice. In P. J. Woods (Ed.), *Career opportunities for psychologists.* Washington, DC: American Psychological Association.

Brooks, R. (1979). Psychoeducational assessment: A broader perspective. *Professional Psychology, 10,* 708–722.

Brown, S. D., & Lent, R. W. (1984). *Handbook of counseling psychology.* New York: John Wiley and Sons.

Burke, M. J., & Normand, J. (1987). Computerized psychological testing: Overview and critique. *Professional Psychology: Research and Practice, 18*, 42–51.

Buros, O. K. (1977). Fifty years in testing: Some reminiscences, criticism, and suggestions. *Educational Researcher, 6*, 9–15.

Carey, M. P., Flasher, L. V., Maisto, S. A., & Turkat, I. D. (1984). The a priori approach to psychological assessment. *Professional Psychology: Research and Practice, 15*, 515–527.

Cleveland, S. E. (1976). Reflections on the rise and fall of psychodiagnosis. *Professional Psychology, 7*, 309–318.

Cole, N. S. (1981). Bias in testing. *American Psychologist, 36*, 1067–1077.

Colliver, J. A., Havens, R. A., & Wesley, R. M. (1985). Doctoral and master's level clinical psychologists and MSWs in public mental health settings: A nationwide follow-up. *Professional Psychology, 16*, 634–640.

Coulter, W. A. (1980). Adaptive behavior and professional disfavor: Controversies and trends for school psychologists. *School Psychology Review, 9*, 67–74.

Coulter, W. A. (1985). Implementing curriculum-based assessment: Considerations for pupil appraisal professionals. *Exceptional Child, 52*, 277–281.

Cranston, A. (1986). Psychology in the Veterans Administration: A storied history, a vital function. *American Psychologist, 41*, 990–995.

Cronbach, L. J. (1975). Five decades of public controversy over mental testing. *American Psychologist, 30*, 1–14.

Cummings, N. (1979, December). The undoing of clinical psychology. *APA Monitor, 2.*

Davids, A. (1973). Projective testing: Some issues facing academicians and practitioners. *Professional Psychology, 4*, 445–453.

Deno, S. L. (1985). Curriculum-based measurement: The emerging alternative. *Exceptional Children, 52*, 219–232.

Dictionary of occupational titles (4th ed.). (1977). Washington, DC: Superintendent of Documents, U.S. Government Printing Office, 49.

Dorken, H. & Associates (Eds.) (1976). *The professional psychologist today.* San Francisco: Jossey-Bass.

Drabman, R. S. (1985). Graduate training of scientist-practitioner-oriented clinical psychologists: Where we can improve. *Professional Psychology: Research and Practice, 16*, 623–633.

DuBois, P. H. (1970). *A history of psychological testing.* Boston: Allyn & Bacon.

Dunnette, M. (Ed.). (1976). *Handbook of industrial and organizational psychology.* Chicago: Rand McNally.

Dunnette, M. D., & Borman, W. C. (1979). Personnel selection and classification systems. *Annual Review of Psychology, 30*, 477–525.

Erdwins, C. J., & Buffardi, L. C. (1983). Employment of recent MAs in psychology: A middle rung on the career ladder. *Professional Psychology: Research and Practice, 14*, 112–117.

Fagan, T. K. (1986). School psychology's dilemma: Reappraising solutions and directing attention to the future. *American Psychologist, 41*, 851–861.

Fee, A. F., Elkins, G. R., & Boyd, L. (1982). Testing and counseling psychologists: Current practices and implications for training. *Journal of Personality Assessment, 46*, 116–118.

Fein, L. G. (Ed.). (1979). Current status of psychological diagnostic testing in university training programs and in delivery of service systems. *Psychological Reports, 44*, 863–879.

Fenster, C. A., Faltico, G., Goldstein, J., Kaslow, F., Locke, B., Musikoff, H., Schlossberg, H., & Wolk, R. (1976). Careers in forensic psychology. In P. J. Woods (Ed.), *Career opportunities for psychologists.* Washington, DC: American Psychological Association.

Fields, F. R. J., & Horwitz, R. J. (Eds.). (1982). *Psychology and professional practice: The interface of psychology and the law.* Westport, CT: Quorum Books.

Fitzgerald, L. F., & Osipow, S. H. (1986). An occupational analysis of counseling psychology: How special is the specialty? *American Psychologist, 41,* 535–544.

Foreman, M. (1977). The changing scene in higher education and the identity of counseling psychology. *The Counseling Psychologist, 7,* 45–48.

Fox, R. E., Kovacs, A. L., & Graham, S. R. (1985). Proposals for a revolution in the preparation and regulation of professional psychologists. *American Psychologist, 40,* 1042–1050.

Fretz, B. R., & Mills, D. H. (1980). *Licensing and certification of psychologists and counselors.* San Francisco: Jossey-Bass.

Fuller, G. B., & Goh, D. S. (1983). Current practices in the assessment of personality and behavior by school psychologists. *School Psychology Review, 12,* 240–243.

Galagan, J. E. (1985). Psychoeducational testing: Turn out the lights, the party's over. *Exceptional Children, 52,* 288–299.

Galassi, J. P., & Moss, N. L. (1986). Training in counseling psychology: 1985 data and trends. *The Counseling Psychologist, 14,* 471–477.

Garfield, S. L., & Kurtz, R. (1976). Clinical psychologists in the 1970s. *American Psychologist, 31,* 1–9.

Gathercole, C. E. (1968). *Assessment in clinical psychology.* Baltimore: Penguin Books.

Glaser, R. (1981). The future of testing: A research agenda for cognitive psychology and psychometrics. *American Psychologist, 36,* 923–936.

Goh, D. S. (1977). Graduate training in school psychology. *Journal of School Psychology, 15,* 207–218.

Goh, D. S., & Fuller, G. B. (1983). Current practices in the assessment of personality and behavior by school psychologists. *School Psychology Review, 12,* 240–243.

Goh, D., Teslow, C. J., & Fuller, G. B. (1981). The practice of psychological assessment among school psychologists. *Professional Psychology, 12,* 696–706.

Goldman, L. (1971). *Using tests in counseling* (2nd ed.). New York: Appleton-Century-Crofts.

Goldschmitt, M., Tipton, R. M., & Wiggins, R. C. (1981). Professional identity of counseling psychologists. *Journal of Counseling Psychology, 28,* 158–167.

Goldstein, A. P., & Krasner, L. (1987). *Modern applied psychology.* Elmsford, NY: Pergamon Press.

Graden, J. L., Casey, A., & Bonstrom, O. (1985). Implementing a prereferral intervention system: Part II. The data. *Exceptional Children, 51,* 487–496.

Graden, J. L., Casey, A., & Christenson, S. L. (1985). Implementing a prereferral intervention system: Part I. The model. *Exceptional Children, 51,* 377–384.

Green, B. F. (1981). A primer of testing. *American Psychologist, 36,* 1001–1011.

Haas, L. J., Malouf, J. L., & Mayerson, N. H. (1986). Ethical dilemmas in psychological practice: Results of a national survey. *Professional Psychology: Research and Practice, 17*(4), 316–321.

Hahn, M. E. (1955). Counseling psychology. *American Psychologist, 10,* 279–282.

Haney, W. (1981). Validity, vaudeville, and values: A short history of social concerns over standardized testing. *American Psychologist, 36,* 1021–1034.

Herr, E. L. (1982). Testing for career counseling, guidance, and education: Reactions to the symposium articles. *Measurement and Evaluation in Guidance, 15,* 159–163.

Hoch, P. H., & Zubin, J. (1955). *Psychiatry and the law.* New York: Grune and Stratton.

Holmes, C. B., Wurtz, P. J., & Waln, R. (1982). Psychology requirements for admission to counseling and counseling psychology programs. *Professional Psychology, 13,* 871–875.

Howard, A. (1982). *Who are the industrial/organizational psychologists? An analysis of data from the 1981 APA directory survey.* Report prepared for the executive committee of Division 14, American Psychological Association.

Howard, A., & Lowman, R. L. (1985). Should industrial/organizational psychologists be licensed? *American Psychologist, 40,* 40–47.

Howard, A., Pion, G. M., Gottfredson, G. D., Flattau, P. E., Oskamp, S., Pfafflin, S. M., Bray, D. W., & Burstein, A. G. (1986). The changing face of American psychology: A report from the committee on employment and human resources. *American Psychologist, 41,* 1311–1327.

Hunter, J. E., Schmidt, I. L. T., & Rauschenberger, J. B. (1977). Fairness of psychological tests: Implications of four definitions for selection utility and minority hiring. *Journal of Applied Psychology, 62,* 245–260.

Ivnik, R. J. (1977). Uncertain status of psychological tests in clinical psychology. *Professional Psychology, 8,* 206–213.

Jeffrey, R. (1964). The psychologist as expert witness on the issue of insanity. *American Psychologist, 19,* 838–843.

Jepsen, D. A. (1982). Test usage in the 1970's: A summary and interpretation. *Measurement and Evaluation in Guidance, 15,* 164–168.

Kane, M. T. (1982). The validity of licensure examinations. *American Psychologist, 37,* 911–918.

Kaplan, R. M., & Saccuzzo, D. P. (1982). *Psychological testing: Principles, applications, and issues.* Monterey, CA: Brooks/Cole.

Keilin, W. G., & Bloom, L. J. (1986). Child custody evaluation practices: A survey of experienced professionals. *Professional Psychology: Research and Practice, 17,* 338–346.

Kellerman, H., & Burry, A. (1981). *Handbook of psychodiagnostic testing: Personality analysis and report writing.* New York: Grune and Stratton.

Kelly, E. L., Goldberg, L. R., Fiske, D. W., & Kilkowski, J. M. (1978). Twenty-five years later: A follow-up study of the graduate students in clinical psychology assessed in the VA selection research project. *American Psychologist, 33,* 746–755.

Keogh, B. K., Kukic, S. J., Becker, L. D., McLoughlin, R. J., & Kukic, M. B. (1975). School psychologists' services in special education programs. *Journal of School Psychology, 13,* 142–148.

Kicklighter, R. H., & Bailey-Richardson, B. (1984). Psychological assessment: Tasks and time. *School Psychology Review, 13,* 499–502.

Kingsbury, S. J. (1987). Cognitive differences between clinical psychologists and psychiatrists. *American Psychologist, 42,* 152–156.

Klatzky, R. L., Alluisi, E. A., Cook, W. A., Forehand, G. A., & Howell, W. C. (1985). Experimental psychologists in industry: Perspectives of employers, employees, and educators. *American Psychologist, 40,* 1031–1037.

Knoff, H. M. (1983a). Personality assessment in the schools: Issues and procedures for school psychologists. *School Psychology Review, 12,* 391–398.

Knoff, H. M. (1983b). Justifying projective/personality assessment in school psychology: A response to Batsche and Peterson. *School Psychology Review, 12,* 446–451.

Korchin, S. J. (1976). *Modern clinical psychology*. New York: Basic Books.

Korchin, S. J., & Schuldberg, D. (1981). The future of clinical assessment. *American Psychologist, 36*, 1147–1158.

Korn, J. H. (1984). New odds on acceptance into Ph.D. programs in psychology. *American Psychologist, 39*, 179–180.

Krumboltz, J. D., Becker-Haven, J. F., & Burnett, K. F. (1979). Counseling psychology. *Annual Review of Psychology, 30*, 555–602.

Kupke, T. (1986). Psychological services provided within Veterans Administration nursing homes. *Professional Psychology: Research and Practice, 17*, 185–190.

Lanyon, R. I. (1986). Psychological assessment procedures in court-related settings. *Professional Psychology: Research and Practice, 17*, 260–268.

Lanyon, R. I., & Goodstein, L. D. (1982). *Personality assessment* (2nd ed.). New York: Wiley.

Levy, L. H. (1984). The metamorphosis of clinical psychology: Toward a new charter as human services psychology. *American Psychologist, 39*, 486–494.

Lewandowski, D. G., & Saccuzzo, D. P. (1976). The decline of psychological testing. *Professional Psychology, 7*, 177–184.

London, M., & Bray, D. W. (1980). Ethical issues in testing and evaluation for personnel decisions. *American Psychologist, 35*, 890–901.

Lubin, B., Larsen, R. M., & Matarazzo, J. D. (1984). Patterns of psychological test usage in the United States: 1935–1982. *American Psychologist, 39*, 451–454.

Lubin, B., Larsen, R. M., Matarazzo, J. D., & Seever, M. F. (1986a). Selected characteristics of psychologists and psychological assessment in five settings: 1959–1982. *Professional Psychology: Research and Practice, 17*, 155–157.

Lubin, B., Larsen, R. M., Matarazzo, J. D., & Seever, M. (1986b). Psychological assessment services and psychological test usage in private practice and in military settings. *Psychotherapy in Private Practice, 4*, 19–29.

Lubin, B., Wallis, R. R., & Paine, C. (1971). Patterns of psychological test usage in the U.S.: 1935–1969. *Professional Psychology, 2*, 70–74.

Manuso, J. S. J. (Ed.). (1983). *Occupational clinical psychology*. New York: Praeger Publishers.

Marquardt, L. D., & McCormick, E. J. (1974). *The job dimensions underlying the job elements of the Position Analysis Questionnaire (PAQ), Form B*. Lafayette, IN: Occupational Research Center, Department of Psychological Sciences, Purdue University, Report No. 4.

McCrae, R. R., & Costa, P. T., Jr. (1986). Clinical assessment can benefit from recent advances in personality psychology. *American Psychologist, 41*, 1001–1003.

Meehl, P. E. (1956). Wanted—a good cookbook. *American Psychologist, 11*, 263–272.

Miller, J. V. (1982). 1970's trends in assessing career counseling, guidance, and education. *Measurement and Evaluation in Guidance, 15*, 142–146.

Miller, K. M. (Ed.). (1975). *Psychological Testing in Personnel Assessment*. New York: John Wiley and Sons.

Mitchell, A. M. (1982). Uses of tests in programs of career guidance and education. *Measurement and Evaluation in Guidance, 15*, 153–158.

Monahan, J. (Ed.). (1980). *Who is the client? The ethics of psychological intervention in the criminal justice system*. Washington, DC: American Psychological Association.

Novick, M. R. (1981). Federal guidelines and professional standards. *American Psychologist, 36*, 1035–1046.

Perlman, B. (1985). Training and career issues of APA-affiliated master-level clinicians. *Professional Psychology: Research and Practice, 16*, 753–767.

Prout, H. T. (1983). School psychologists and social-emotional assessment techniques: Patterns in training and use. *School Psychology Review, 12,* 377–383.

Pruitt, J. A., Smith, M. C., Thelen, M. H., & Lubin, B. (1985). Attitudes of academic clinical psychologists toward projective techniques: 1968–1983. *Professional Psychology: Research and Practice, 16,* 781–788.

Randolph, D. L. (1979). The sleeping giant awakens. *APA Division of Community Psychology Newsletter, 12,* 14–15.

Reschly, D. J. (1981). Psychological testing in educational classification and placement. *American Psychologist, 36,* 1094–1102.

Reynolds, C. R., & Elliott, S. N. (1983). Trends in development and publication of educational psychological tests. *Professional Psychology: Research and Practice, 14,* 554–558.

Rosen, R. H. (1983). The need for training in forensic child psychology. *Professional Psychology: Research and Practice, 14,* 481–489.

Saccuzzo, D. P., & Schulte, R. H. (1978). The value of a terminal master's degree for Ph.D. pursuing students in psychology. *American Psychologist, 33,* 862–864.

Schaefer, C. E., Briesmeister, J. M., & Fitton, M. E. (1984). *Family therapy techniques for problem behaviors of children and teenagers.* San Francisco: Jossey-Bass.

Scheirer, C. J. (1983). Professional schools: Information for students and advisors. *Teaching of Psychology, 10,* 11–15.

Schmidt, F. L., & Hunter, J. E. (1981). Employment testing: Old theories and new research findings. *American Psychologist, 36,* 1128–1137.

Schultz, D. P. (1978). *Psychology and industry today* (2nd ed.). New York: Macmillan.

Schultz, D. P., & Schultz, S. E. (1986). *Psychology and industry today* (4th ed.). New York: Macmillan.

Seime, R. J., McCauley, R. L., & Madsen, R. K. (1977). Comparing interview impressions and test results: A new test interpretation format and procedure. *Professional Psychology, 8,* 199–205.

Shakow, D. (1976). What is clinical psychology? *American Psychologist, 31,* 553–560.

Shakow, D. (1978). Clinical psychology seen some 50 years later. *American Psychologist, 33,* 148–158.

Shellenberger, S. (1982). Presentation and interpretation of psychological data in educational settings. In C. R. Reynolds & T. B. Gutkin (Eds.), *The handbook of school psychology.* New York: John Wiley and Sons.

Shimberg, B. (1981). Testing for licensing and certification. *American Psychologist, 36,* 1138–1146.

Shimberg, E. (1979). *The handbook of private practice in psychology.* New York: Brunner/ Mazel.

Siegel, L., & Lane, I. M. (1982). *Personnel and organizational psychology.* Homewood, IL: Richard D. Irwin.

Skinner, H. A., & Pakula, A. (1986). Challenge of computers in psychological assessment. *Professional Psychology: Research and Practice, 17,* 44–50.

Smith, D. (1982). Trends in counseling and psychotherapy. *American Psychologist, 37,* 802–809.

Standards for educational and psychological testing. (1985). Washington, DC: American Psychological Association.

Stapp, J., Fulcher, R., & Wicherski, M. (1984). The employment of 1981 and 1982 doctorate recipients in psychology. *American Psychologist, 39,* 1408–1423.

Stapp, J., Tucker, A. M., & VandenBos, G. R. (1985). Census of psychological personnel: 1983. *American Psychologist, 40*, 1317–1351.

Stoup, C. M., & Benjamin, L. T. (1982). Graduate study in psychology, 1970–1979. *American Psychologist, 37*, 1186–1202.

Sundberg, N. D. (1961). The practice of psychological testing in clinical service in the United States. *American Psychologist, 16*, 79–83.

Sundberg, N. D. (1977). *Assessment of persons.* Englewood Cliffs, NJ: Prentice-Hall.

Super, C. M., & Super, D. E. (1982). *Opportunities in psychology.* Lincolnwood, IL: National Textbook Co.

Tenopyr, M. L. (1981). The realities of employment testing. *American Psychologist, 36*, 1120–1127.

Thelen, M. H., & Ewing, D. R. (1970). Roles, functions, and training in clinical psychology: A survey of academic clinicians. *American Psychologist, 25*, 550–554.

Tucker, J. A. (1985). Curriculum-based assessment: An introduction. *Exceptional Children, 52*, 199–204.

Ulrich, L., & Trumbo, D. (1965). The selection interview since 1949. *Psychological Bulletin, 63*, 100–116.

Wade, T. C., & Baker, T. B. (1977). Opinions and use of psychological tests. *American Psychologist, 32*, 874–882.

Wade, T. C., Baker, T. B., Morton, T. L., & Baker, L. J. (1978). The status of psychological testing in clinical psychology: Relationships between test use and professional activities and orientations. *Journal of Personality Assessment, 42*, 3–10.

Ware, M. E. (1984). Helping students to evaluate areas of graduate study in psychology. *College Student Journal, 18*, 2–11.

Ware, M. E., & Meyer, A. E. (1981). Career versatility of the psychology major: A survey of graduates. *Teaching of Psychology, 8*, 12–15.

Watkins, C. E. (1985). Counseling psychology, clinical psychology, and human services psychology: Where the twain shall meet? *American Psychologist, 40*, 1054–1056.

Watkins, C. E. (1983). Counseling psychology versus clinical psychology. *The Counseling Psychologist, 11*, 76–92.

Watkins, C. E. (1984). Reflections on the roles and functions of counseling psychologists. *Professional Psychology, 15*, 472–475.

Watkins, C. E., Lopez, F. G., Campbell, V. L., & Himmell, C. D. (1986). Counseling psychology and clinical psychology: Some preliminary comparative data. *American Psychologist, 41*, 581–582.

Weigel, R. (1977). I have seen the enemy and they is us—and everyone else. *The Counseling Psychologist, 7*, 50-53.

Wesman, A. G. (1968). Intelligent testing. *American Psychologist, 23*, 267–274.

West, P. R., & Lips, O. J. (1986). Veterans Administration psychology: A professional challenge for the 1980s. *American Psychologist, 41*, 996–1000.

Williams, M. (1965). *Mental testing in clinical practice.* Oxford: Pergamon Press.

Wise, P. S., Smith, G. F., & Fulkerson, F. E. (1983). Occupations of psychology majors receiving undergraduate degrees from Western Illinois University. *Teaching of Psychology, 10*, 53–54.

Woods, P. J. (1976). *Career opportunities for psychologists: Expanding and emerging areas.* Washington, DC: American Psychological Association.

Woods, P. J. (1979). *The psychology major: Training and employment strategies.* Washington, DC: American Psychological Association.

Zook, A. (1987). On the merger of clinical and counseling psychology. *Professional Psychology: Research and Practice, 18,* 4–5.

Zytowski, D. G., & Warman, R. E. (1982). The changing use of tests in counseling. *Measurement and Evaluation in Guidance, 15,* 147–152.

Index

day treatment programs, 43
diagnostic model, 27
Diana v. State of California, 111
Dictionary of Occupational Titles, 69
disabled, 14, 29, 33, 130. *See also*
    handicapped
displaced homemakers, 40
Draw-A-Person Test, 38, 120

EdD degree, 19
EdS degree, 20
educable mentally retarded (EMR), 111
educational psychology, 17
Edwards Personal Preference Schedule,
    56, 134
employee evaluation, 82–83
engineering psychology, 26
entry-level degree, 18–21
ethical issues in testing, 1, 10, 49, 65, 83,
    84, 105, 106, 116–118
etiology, 104
expectancy effects, 7
expert witness, 114

family therapy, 35, 42
    Family Portraits, 37
    Family Sculptures, 37
Fee, A. F., 55, 56, 139
Fenster, C. A., 109, 139
follow-up, 4, 13, 28, 77, 96
forced-choice measures, 42
Foreman, M., 25, 139
formulation of questions/hypotheses, 3,
    28, 92
Fox, R. E., 29, 139
Fretz, B. R., 20, 139

Garfield, S. L., 23, 139
gerontology, 63, 64
gifted and talented, 2, 29
Goldman, L., 54, 56, 57, 139
Goldschmitt, M., 53, 139
Goldstein, A. P., 72, 139
Goodenough-Harris Drawing Test, 120,
    134
Graden, J. L., 106, 139
Graduate Record Examination (GRE),
    77, 134
*Graduate Study in Psychology and
    Associated Fields,* 21, 30
Griggs v. Duke Power Co., 112

group tests, 1, 2, 28
*Guadalupe v. Tempe Elementary
    District,* 111

Halstead-Reitan Neuropsychological
    Battery, 46, 134
handicapped, 2, 89, 90. *See also* disabled
health history, 46, 92, 103
High School Equivalency Exam (GED),
    35
Hobson v. Hanson, 111, 112
Holmes, C. B., 25, 140
House-Tree-Person Technique, 38, 134
Howard, A., 26, 140
human factors, 85
human service areas, 29
hyperactivity, 8
hypothesis formation, 4

in-basket exercises, 75
individually administered tests, 1, 2
industrial/organizational (I/O) psychol-
    ogy, 14, 18, 20, 21, 26, 27, 67–86,
    130
informal assessment, 37
informed consent, 101
inservice workshops, 29
intake forms, 4
integration of information, 12
intelligence testing, 1, 111, 112
interest inventories, 1
interpersonal communication skills, 12,
    69
interpretation of test results, 2, 3, 10, 95,
    123
intervention plan, 12
interviews, 4–6, 13, 27, 71, 72, 82, 90, 92,
    94, 114, 115, 122

Kaplan, R. M., 113, 140
Keilin, W. G., 115, 140
Kingsbury, S. J., 23, 140
Kuder Occupational Interest Survey, 56,
    134

labor relations, 27
Larry P. v. Riles, 112, 129
learning disability (LD), 61, 130
legal issues, 109–116, 129
letters of recommendation, 7, 71–73